MARATHON MINDSET

Outrun the Voice of Negativity

By: **Rekha Gibbons**

Copyright © 2026 Rekha Gibbons. All rights reserved.

No part of this publication may be reproduced, distributed, or transmitted in any form or by any means, including photocopying, recording, or other electronic or mechanical methods, without the prior written permission of the author. Brief excerpts may be used for purposes such as critical reviews or other non-commercial uses permitted by copyright law provided that full and proper attribution is given to the author, Rekha Gibbons.

For permission requests, please contact the author directly at:

Rekha Gibbons
Email: rekhagibbons@gmail.com
Website: https://rekhagibbons.com/
ISBN: 9798995486701

THE EXPERTS WEIGH IN – ACCLAIM FOR MARATHON MINDSET: OUTRUN THE VOICE OF NEGATIVITY

Brian Tracy, Author of Eat That Frog! and Maximum Achievement

"Marathon Mindset: Outrun the Voice of Negativity is a powerpacked manual for peak performance. Pinpointing our 'voice of negativity' as our chief limiter, Rekha Gibbons delivers clear, actionable tactics to silence it. Beyond theory, she lays out a step by step blueprint for forging the mental toughness to not just finish life's race but win it. If you're serious about limitless achievement, this is an indispensable guide that will transform your mindset and unleash your unstoppable self."

Marshall Ulrich, Legendary Ultrarunner & Endurance Icon, Author of Running on Empty

"Rekha Gibbons gets it. The real race isn't on the pavement; it's between your ears. Marathon Mindset: Outrun the Voice of Negativity digs deep into the grit, the resilience, and the sheer will it takes to push past your limits. If you want to truly understand what you're made of – and that it's more than you think – read this book. It's the real deal."

Kelly Lynn Adams, Business & Life Coach Catalyst

"Rekha Gibbons hasn't just written a book—she's delivered a manifesto for the modern leader. Marathon Mindset: Outrun the Voice of Negativity is the permission slip you need to stop settling for a life designed by someone else's limits. In her gorgeous and hilarious voice, Rekha breaks down the bottom line in this high-stakes race called life. She doesn't offer soft, fluffy advice; she hands you the blueprint for mental domination, proving that the only difference between a burned-out consumer and a thriving, high-performer is a single, strategic shift in mindset.

This book is a Catalyst. It forces you to look at your life and ask, "Am I being an Owner of my trajectory, or merely a Consumer of others' demands?" Marathon Mindset gives you the tools to silence the internal noise and step onto the track of true self-mastery. You determine how far you go, how much you win, and how much joy you keep in the process. This book is the game-changer that makes all of that possible. Read it. Live it. Win your life back."

Lisa Davies, (nee Whitehead), Author of Get a Life – The Guidebook

"Marathon Mindset: Outrun the Voice of Negativity is more than a book; it's a lifeline for anyone who's ever battled the relentless voice of self-doubt. Rekha writes with the wisdom of a leader, the compassion of a healer and the courage of someone who has walked (and run) through the fire herself. This is not just about outrunning negativity; it's about reclaiming your mind, your power and your joy. If you're ready to meet the strongest, most resilient version of yourself, this is your starting line."

By Kevin Baltzer, 10x plus Marathon Finisher, Boston & New York

Rekha Gibbons's Marathon Mindset is the best training partner you'll ever have. Rekha is a world class writer–vivid, fun, carrying the perfect tempo of a seasoned runner. She doesn't just cover the miles; she dissects the true marathon—the one happening inside your head. This book is a brilliant field guide to winning that inner race, offering a concrete toolkit for tackling the crippling self-doubt at Mile 17 and transforming the pain cave into a necessary mile marker. A must-read for runners and non-runners alike! We all need more peace of mind in the chaotic journey of life.

DEDICATION

To Wayne, my coach, companion, my favorite person. Thank you for co-creating our glorious movie. I can't wait for our next adventure.

PREFACE: ABOUT THAT LITTLE VOICE IN YOUR HEAD...

It was March 2024, and I'd been hearing it for a while. My clients, my colleagues, bless their earnest, well-meaning hearts, kept insisting, "Rekha, seriously, people need to see you. That's where the impact, the real magic happens. It's time you electrified the screen."

It had been 7 months since I left my C-Suite role at a Marketing Agency. After spending thirty-five years navigating the corporate grind, I hit a glorious, undeniable wall. The one that tells you it's time for a major-league reinvention. So, I ditched the peep-toe pumps, tossed out the boy's club playbook, and became a full-blown Corporate Hired Gun. My mission? To hammer through the revolving door of conflict and turnover, making five generations in the workplace not just coexist, but actually sing in harmony like Glee on steroids.

Look, I've been immersed for decades on the marketing and tech rollercoaster—from clunky typewriters to mind-bending AI. I've witnessed the birth of the Internet, watched the digital marketing explosion, survived 911, queasily observed social media's takeover, and agonized when venerable financial institutions went down in flames in 2008 (taking my 401k with them, middle finger raised). I've amassed a truckload of wisdom, and it was crystal clear: It was time to pay it forward. To unleash all that hard-won wisdom and help other fierce souls not just build rewarding careers but create flat-out epic lives.

The mission didn't just resonate—it detonated. Companies swarmed, lining up like groupies for me to ignite their events and deliver transformative workshops. Simultaneously, universities came knocking, eager for me to spill the unvarnished truth on what students really needed to expect from that glorious, chaotic thing called a job. From there, I didn't just speak to companies; I hit the big leagues: landing national TV spots, dominating major conference stages, mic-dropping on top podcasts, and commanding industry summits. Gratefully, everyone wanted a piece of the action, validating my insight as the 'Generational Guru'.

The Video Plunge & Manhattan Dreams

So, like the brave soul I like to think I am, I took the plunge into the untamed jungle of video. This isn't Martha Quinn's MTV; we're talking a world dominated by short-form, instantly shareable, easy-to-binge content. Outside my comfort zone – big time. So, I hired a super cute millennial named Georgiy – I can say that because I'm twice his age, and it's a sign of the times, this cross-generational collaboration. This young gun, a master of social posting, brought a whole different kind of genius to the table. We set an ambitious timeline for a late May shoot, and he laid out the blueprint: title, body, call to action—the bare-bones essentials of a message that actually permeates in less than 60 seconds. Now, I'm usually all about the sprawling narratives, the epic sagas of longer formats, but I embraced the challenge. And? We cranked out nine killer short videos and a sizzle reel, all custom-built to crystallize my personal brand and services.

The shoot itself was a masterclass in contrasts: a swanky, industrial-style studio in the heart of NYC, with rooftop vistas that practically screamed Manhattan Dreams! A small, crack team—videographer, photographer, a makeup artist and the studio owner—all came together to capture my unfiltered essence.

I like to think I'm comfortable in front of an audience. But let me tell you, that's a whole different beast when you're staring down the barrel of a video lens. It's not just about what you say, but *how* you say it. I had to learn 'camera face'— that subtle, almost magical art of radiating pure energy and authenticity without looking like you're about to pop a blood vessel or go full mime. It's a discipline, this less is more thing, especially when you're trying to amplify your message without looking like you're flagging down a plane. And my hands? Seriously, it's nearly impossible for me to speak without waving like I'm conducting the Boston Pops. My cousin actually timed me in church once, just to see how long I could talk without using my hands. I lasted less than 8 seconds. True story.

The shoot, by all accounts, went well. I nailed most of the videos faster than you can say "neuroplasticity" and crucially, I connected with the crew. The makeup artist Wray, who does Vogue shoots – yeah, that level – was captivated by one video in particular: "The Most Important Relationship You Will Ever Have Is With Yourself." During the filming she sat on the sofa, watching me with this intense, laser focus. Later, she pulled me aside and told me, "This is such an important message. The world needs to hear this." By the way, we're Instagram pals now.

We wrapped the shoot, even grabbing some killer rooftop shots. Awesome. It's Reel time, baby! That evening? A full-on celebration. My hubby and I toasted with our favorite bubbly and indulged in a festive dinner. Cranking out intensely weighty content, performing for the camera, projecting the energy and vitality that matches the message—it's draining, sure. But it's also deeply, profoundly satisfying. Exhaustion and contentment settled in like old friends.

The Unholy Wake-up Call

And then, the vulnerability. The 2:30 AM wake-up call. A voice, nasty as an evil hangover, whispered in my head – "Now you've done it. You've shown the world who you really are, and they're going to hate you."

I laid there, bathed in the baleful aqua glow of the digital clock, thinking, "WTF? Who *was* that voice?" I mean, I've done the work for heaven's sake. Self-awareness, subconscious reprogramming, personal empowerment – the whole shebang. I've immersed myself for decades in this stuff – metaphysics, self-improvement, personal transformation, learning from luminaries like the ethereal Abraham Hicks to the preacher enthusiasm of Zig Ziglar. I thought I'd dealt with imposter syndrome, vanquished it into the long distant past. So, where the hell did *that voice* come from?

The next day, my mind was just a mess. A total pinball machine of negativity. I went through my usual morning routine – stretches, coffee with a scoop of collagen, walking Sonny our three-legged rescue dog. Things that usually ground me, fill me with joy, along with precious doggy kisses. But not that day. My mind was just ricocheting from one thought to another, each more irrational than the last. It was as if my mind was a map, you could see these tendrils of anxiety spreading out, connecting one worst-case scenario to the next. What if I looked stupid in those videos?

What if the reels got zero likes? Worse, what if they *did* get attention, but all of it negative? Hateful comments, you know, lashing out at my message, my appearance, my persona. I shuddered.

And then, as if on cue, the universe seemed to reflect the fear and negativity I was wrestling with internally. The world outside seemed to be wailing it everywhere. 80% of Americans reported having negative thoughts. The relentless news cycle, with its unwavering focus on conflict, division, and bleak outcomes felt overwhelming. It was like humanity was tied into a constant drip-feed of stress and despair. People felt powerless, their voices unheard. Clashes over deeply held values, causing emotional distress, anger, frustration. There was even a new phrase: "Election Stress Disorder". Yes, it's a real thing, not just an AI hallucination.

The Dragon of Negativity

It felt like the whole world was feeling the same intense anxiety I was. The dragon was real, and it wasn't just in my head. And it wasn't just some abstract sense of doom. The year was marked by significant political and social upheaval, leading to a widespread reevaluation of long-standing business and community initiatives. That whole chaotic mess threw me a brutal curveball.

Just when things were humming along, engaging with two seriously important clients—one a government agency, the other a global management consultancy—teaching Leadership, Resilience, and Peak Performance, the universe decided to throw a wrench in my plans. A new administration swept in, and just like that, both clients pulled the plug on our projects almost overnight.

"We're sorry," they said. "We love what you do, but our funding and strategic priorities have been reallocated." Decades of building my reputation, all that hard-won corporate experience, my institutional knowledge—poof! Vanished in a single month. It was a sudden, totally unexpected gut-punch that demanded a full reassessment. Not just of my business, but of my entire purpose.

And that's when it truly struck me how incredibly, fundamentally unfair it is that a single errant thought, a little brain fart of negativity, can hijack a day, month, even year triggering this avalanche of self-sabotaging thinking.

The voice of negativity in my head wasn't just whispering anymore; it was screaming at death-metal volume. At times, I honestly felt like I was losing my mind. People who know me consider me the eternal optimist. Matter of fact, during COVID, I changed my title from Chief Operating Officer to Chief Optimism Officer. Where was that uplifting person now? She'd clearly taken a vacation in a galaxy far, far away.

Your Brain, Your Worst Frenemy

If you're reading this, you're probably already wrestling with your own version of that inner critic. That annoying little jerk-face who murmurs that you're a total mess, a colossal failure, or a Loser with a capital L. The voice that's got a VIP pass to all your insecurities and plays them on a never-ending, soul-crushing loop. Yeah, that's your brain, bless its overthinking heart, running some seriously old, outdated software.

The Trap

Because here's the kicker: We're living in a world that, on the surface, feels custom-designed to fuel your inner dragon. We're wired for genuine connection, right? But the very tools we clutch onto so tightly can also make us feel more alone, more inadequate, more utterly consumed by the dreamy curated perfection of others. Reality shows aren't real. We've become a society utterly obsessed with peeking into other people's lives, drawn to the Jerry Springer-esque drama, convinced that someone else's highlight reel is inherently better, more fun, more exciting than our own messy, beautiful reality. That illusion we buy into—those fun, silly selfie posts where she looks so dewy or he is so damn ripped—they're manufactured, baby. It takes a whole lot of time and some moolah to create that "effortless" life. Why are we so keen to pay attention to their reels while neglecting our own unfolding, utterly unique story?

This isn't just about feeling a bit down. This relentless negativity, this constant comparison, this feeling of powerlessness? It's literally rewiring your brain. It's building neural superhighways for dread and self-doubt. It's keeping you small, safe, and frankly, bored. It's stealing your joy, dimming your light, and robbing you of the vibrant, heroic life you were born to live.

The Vow

In the middle of that very real, very ugly struggle, a tiny spark flickered. A realization dawned in me: If I could conquer this crushing wave of negativity, if I could get my Chief Optimism Officer back on duty, then dang it, so could YOU.

So, I made a commitment. A fierce, whispered oath to the universe, loud enough for my soul to hear: "Show me how to tame this negative voice, and I'll show others how to do the same thing."

Word of caution, Tonto: When you make a vow like that, buckle up and beware. You don't just open a door to another portal; you unleash a bronco-bucking, wild-ass ride that'll challenge every ounce of your being.

I dove headfirst into researching every possible avenue to contend with this negativity: the brilliant minds in neuroscience and psychology, the mind-bending frequencies of subconscious reprogramming, the ancient wisdom whispered through Mystery Schools, a plethora of resources from teachings old and new, the vast reservoir of the Internet, and even the cutting-edge insights blinked up by AI.

What I started seeing was nothing short of revolutionary: a whole new way of perceiving the human mindset. How to utterly challenge our preconceived notions of what truly causes happiness and, conversely, what fuels that gnawing negativity. How humans are so deeply, intricately connected to each other, whether we realize it or not. And how evolution, bless its methodical heart, takes its own sweet time. While human technology has escalated at warp speed since the 1800s—from Agrarian farming to the dizzying Age of Technology—our emotional and psychological development has not caught up to that blazing pace. Our brains are still running on software designed for survival in the savanna, not for surviving your Twitter feed... pardon me, I mean X feed.

THE REVELATION: THE MARATHON MINDSET

Then, like a lightning bolt from the cosmos, a random comment from my husband, who's run a mind-boggling 350+ marathons–a master at bending reality with his mind — echoed in my head:

> *"If you're going to run a marathon, you better be really good friends with your mind. Because for miles and miles, that's all you've got."*

Kaboom! The realization hit me like a thunderbolt. What did he, and other wacky people who consistently push past perceived limits, know that I didn't? That epiphany blasted open a whole new door for me. One in which I came to explore a swifter, purer, and ultimately more primal approach to mental mastery.

Most of us will never win Olympic gold medal, never give an Oscar acceptance speech, never rock MetLife Stadium with a sold-out show. But every single one of us has the seed of a hero–a valiant superhero–within us. We all secretly yearn to be that larger-than-life version of ourselves, in our own unique and glorious way. And running long distances—or frankly any consistent disciplined effort that pushes your boundaries— allows us to absolutely smash through our own personal limitations. We're talking shattering the chains of both your body and your brilliant brain.

Your Roadmap to a Resilient Mind

That moment of clarity is exactly what led me to write Marathon Mindset: Outrun the Voice of Negativity. This book isn't about fluffy affirmations; it's about rewiring your brain.

You will learn how to fundamentally transform your negative mindset—that noisy, self-sabotaging inner critic—into its natural, inherent state: one of unshakeable confidence, fierce self-nurturing, and radical self-love.

You will unearth the powerful secret known by runners, philosophers, and truth-seekers for centuries: **Your Mind is Yours to Control**. Mastering this control is the absolute, non-negotiable key to unlocking your fiercest, most joyful, and profoundly peaceful reality.

Inside You Will Discover:

The Master Switch: Victim to Transformer

Claim the undeniable power of your mind and learn to silence the inner critic that fuels self-doubt. You are the master of your destiny, not a victim of your thoughts.

Runner's Resilience Blueprint

Unlock the powerful, primal tools runners use to push mental boundaries, overcome pain, and find profound joy in the moment.

Break the Echo Chamber

Evolve past the limiting tribal mindset and stop living by other people's outdated rules and collective self-sabotage.

Neuroscience for Rewiring

Understand the groundbreaking science of neuroplasticity: how your brain can literally rewire its negative patterns for lasting, positive change.

Owner vs. Consumer Mentality

Reclaim your most precious resources—your time, energy, and focus—and invest them aggressively in the life you truly want to create.

Nature's Emotional Reset

Discover the radical, immediate power of nature and how simply connecting with the natural world can shift negativity into a state of profound calm.

Amplify the Win

Train your brain to seek out and celebrate every victory, big and small, reinforcing the neural pathways for happiness and success.

You'll get killer insights from the gurus who've truly mastered their game—both professionally and personally. We'll also pay homage to the trailblazers–the visionaries and old-school legends who didn't just make running a sport, but a whole lifestyle. You'll discover how this incredible movement evolved, soak up inspiration from the luminaries who set the pace, and uncover how their timeless basics are still the no-BS blueprint for unstoppable success.

Think of it as the ultimate upgrade for your most valuable asset: your brain. An upgrade that allows you to unlock your full potential by learning to face life's curveballs with an empowered, confident mindset.

Bonus: Trading Rackets for Resilience

I'm also going to spill the beans on how I traded in my graphite tennis racket for a bona fide marathoner badge. I'll take you through the most brutal and beautiful running landscapes on Earth: from the desolate volcanic fields of Kona to the glacial peaks of the French Alps, and up to the thin, 14,000-foot air of the Colorado Rockies.

We'll splash through Kauai—the wettest place on Earth—scale the majestic alpine paths of the John Muir trail, and fly down the stunning coast of Maui.

I'll share all the gritty lessons learned, like why you absolutely, positively must wear shoes two sizes bigger when running marathons. (Trust me, tight sneakers cause toenails to fall off. You're welcome.)

Think of this book as an invitation to embark on a kick-ass journey of self-discovery and transformation. To break free from the invisible shackles of negativity and embrace a life of clarity, resilience, and unapologetic purpose.

So, get ready to be challenged, in the best way! To be inspired, get your tissues ready, sometimes it's emotional. And to discover the incredible capacity for change that lies within you. The future of your mind, and perhaps the future of your entire life, is in your hands.

Are you ready to tame your own dragon of negativity? Are you prepared to make your mind your friend, not your worst enemy? Are you ready to learn how to reprogram your mind to do your will, and not just follow the tired, old program it's been running on autopilot? Are you ready to stop consuming the negativity, the drama, the comparison, and finally take ownership? Of your mind, your joy, and your peace?

Then let's get running. You magnificent creature, you.

TABLE OF CONTENTS

CHAPTER 1

WHAT IF YOUR LIFE WAS A MOVIE?

My Childhood Reel

Growing up, my personal movie was a silent film titled: Bookworm Who Craves Adventure.

My childhood was an atypical immigrant Indian saga—less Slumdog Millionaire, more WASP from the Subcontinent. My private Christian schooling meant a heavy curriculum of Protestant theology, deep study of the scriptures, and enough of the Book of Revelations to make you perpetually brace for the End of the World. The structure was rigid, but my mind was restless. I yearned for action, for unfamiliar experiences, for exotic expeditions.

But here's the kicker: my life never matched my dreams. Things just seemed to get in the way: rigid familial beliefs, crushing societal pressure, and the omnipresent, suffocating weight of expectation. While the Adventurous Heroine was clawing to get out, the polite Good Girl was following the well-worn path: singing in the choir, crushing spelling bees, and living the pristine, almost alarmingly well-behaved life of a teenage Desi.

In the midst of this obedience, my own antihero offered some delightful self-perceptions: I didn't look like the person I wanted to be. My hair was too curly (a curly-haired girl knows the struggle). My eyebrows were so aggressive they practically had their own zip code and I was definitely not super model height. General lack of chutzpah meant I couldn't open my mouth, let alone star in my own life. I was living a polite life when I craved an exciting one.

My world, however, was anchored by love and joyful chaos. My parents practically put me on a pedestal—sweet, but not exactly a launching pad for a future spy thriller protagonist. This pedestal was surrounded by a massive extended family: twenty-nine cousins, most of whom were my ride-or-die best friends.

Academically, I was a total bookworm. My uncanny knack for English was noticed early—my first-grade teacher, Mrs. Lundsford, appointed me her student assistant to help my American scholars with grammar. Go figure. In my secret, wilder moments, I'd scribble poetry and send it off to the Blue Mountain greeting card company, convinced they would recognize my nascent talent and hire me on the spot. (Spoiler alert: they did not. But a girl can dream.)

When it came to sports, I was all about fast-twitch muscles, not stamina. I never yearned to run across Death Valley or climb Everest. Luckily, I found my perfect sport at age seven: Tennis. The short, turbo bursts and the satisfying gestalt of the racket suited me perfectly.

Beneath all that obedience, a fierce craving brewed. I knew there was a "more" to me, something bolder, something that didn't involve being polite—but I had no damn idea what that "more" looked like.

The Unshakeable Lead Actress

I yearned to be like super spy, Mrs. Emma Peel. Remember her from the 1960s British show the Avengers? The *Original* Avengers. She was played by Diana Rigg, who, incidentally, has the distinction of being the one and ONLY Mrs. James Bond. Mrs. Peel rocked a skintight leather catsuit that made jaws drop. She was this suave contrast of posh femininity and martial arts pizazz, serving up ass-kicking with a side of dry British wit. Teenage boys crushed on her, even better, she influenced a whole generation of girls, Moi included. I didn't know it at the time, but this woman was a force for equality. She fought hard for equal pay as an actress – because apparently, the cameraman made more money than she did. Eye roll.

All I knew then was that she was urbane, self-possessed, and unbelievably comfortable in her own skin. Ah, that was it. What I admired about her was she was her own woman, and she not only liked it, she reveled in it!

Passage to Epiphany

The universe, in its own infinite wisdom, finally answered the Adventurous Hero's demand. After thirteen years, our family was making the passage home—a journey my parents had been pining for since our departure in 1969. An aunt's wedding provided the magnetic pull, a massive cultural anchor dropping into our predictable suburban lives.

I wasn't returning home; I was embarking on the first true adventure I'd only dreamed about. I was tickled to return to the motherland, a place I recalled through misty nostalgia.

I still remember the glorious chaos that assaulted us at the New Delhi airport. Families, looking like they were towing entire villages worth of luggage, swarmed in disorderly clusters. Scrawny men, yelling "Taxiwala, taxiwala!" like a battle cry, lunged to grab your suitcase and wrestle it into a waiting taxi. Dad, in his element, expertly negotiated a price, and we all squished inside. That taxi driver, bless his heart, became our personal chauffeur for the entire trip, shuttling us from one sooty village to another. Any notion of driving ourselves was instantly shattered the moment we saw the streets – a living, breathing mêlée of cars, trucks, scooters, all dodging and weaving between humans and livestock.

And the cows! Oh my goodness, the cows and bullocks just sauntered through the streets like they owned the place. Which, I guess, they kind of did, since cows are sacred in India! Then there were the stray dogs – lean and brown, with wiry tails and ribs poking out like bony armor, their eyes bright black like polished onyx. Our driver commanded the wheel of India's undisputed car of choice from the 50s to the mid-80s: the Ambassador. It was a compact four-door sedan that somehow, uncomfortably, swallowed our family of four: Mom, Dad, my brother, and me.

Our driver navigated us through villages that smelled like burnt chestnuts – a strangely comforting scent that reminded me of New York City at Christmas. He'd nonchalantly overtake buses from which arms, legs, and the occasional chicken spilled out of the windows with a death-wish intensity. Stringy, inquisitive boys with slicked-back black hair would stare at our car, their hands reaching out as we walked by, softly begging, "Amma, Amma?" (Please lady, please miss.)

We did the rounds of family visits, which meant endless, elaborate meals served on rustic but charming, massive banana leaves that lasted for hours. Distant cousins I'd never met, relatives removed by two, three, even more degrees – all of them absolutely thrilled to see "the kids from America."

And then there were the girls. My age. Stunningly beautiful. Girls with cheekbones that would make an Eastern European supermodel weep with envy. Glossy black hair that seemed to absorb all the light, defiant lips that held untold stories, and bodies draped in half-saris of brightly colored georgette, wrapped around slender, brown torsos. Their fitted cotton blouses still sported that old-school stitching, a cheeky nod to those bullet bras from the 60s. It was like stepping right into a 1960s time warp!

And it hit me with a gut punch: Surely these girls are destined for nothing more than the same old, tired narrative: marry, toil, and propagate the soul-crushing cycle once again. And here I was, wasting the freedom I had been handed, complaining that my hair was frizzy.

That experience tattooed itself onto my soul. It was the earth-shattering epiphany I needed: I could live any freaking life I wanted. I had all the options, all the abilities, and all the privileges, and I had been letting them collect dust, like an undiscovered treasure.

From that exact moment, I stopped making excuses for what I was not. And I started playing with the concept of creating my own movie. A blockbuster, starring me. I started creating my own reality, shaping exactly what I wanted to BE.

It was as if the world cracked open in front of me like an enchanted book, and I could suddenly see all the wild, exhilarating paths I could take. And I was just infused with this overwhelming wave of gratitude. For my family, for my health, athleticism, for my brain and all the crazy, brilliant things it conjured. Because in that moment I gave myself permission. Permission to stop taking myself for granted, to stop dimming my own light, and to finally embrace who and what I really was. Permission to live a life that gave me an excited, roaring purpose. Permission to break away from all the

BS, all the soul-sucking expectations, all the things that held me back from being authentically, unapologetically ME.

The Big Question: Whose Movie Are You Living?

Let's cut to the chase, because this right here is the crux of this entire book.

Have you ever stopped to think of your life as a movie? Not just a random documentary of your existence with grainy black and white footage, but a full-blown, lights-camera-action, Hollywood-style flick? Seriously, what would it be? A nail-biting Thriller? A heartwarming Rom-Com? Or, God forbid, a Tragedy that makes everyone reach for the tissues?

I want you to really think about your life right now as a movie. What's the story you're currently spinning about who you are, about what's even possible for your magnificent self? Is it the movie you want to be in, or are you just some bit player in someone else's rehashed script? Are you creating the reality, the blockbuster you truly desire?

The stuff we believe, the things we just blindly take for granted – they are not just random thoughts. Oh no. They are the invisible, unbreakable threads that weave the entire fabric of your current existence and, more importantly, your future. Your happiness, your feelings, your undeniable power – you think they're just "out there," floating around like a lucky break? Nope. Every single one of them, without exception, is absolutely within grasp of your earnest hands.

And what if you were the writer of your own script? Or even better, the Director? Would you be Ridley Scott, meticulously crafting every scene of your life with a combo of science and humanity? Or how about this for a mind-blower: If your life was a movie, who would play the hero? If Timothée Chalamet was starring in your life, do you honestly think he'd just sit around whining about the traffic? Or Halle Berry – she wouldn't complain about her hair, right? She'd just kick some serious butt and dazzle the screen. Get my drift?

Here's the million-dollar question: What's holding you back? What will it take to finally slap yourself silly and give yourself permission to live the life of your wildest dreams? Because, let me be crystal clear, it's exactly that –

the life you dream. And that Oscar-worthy premiere? It's not happening unless you give it the one thing it needs: Belief.

But there's a catch, because of course, there has to be. You have to truly believe two fundamental rules in order for them to actually come to fruition. What, pray tell, are they? Well, buckle up, buttercup. That's why you're here.

Let's lay down the first commandment of your new, Marathon Mindset existence. This isn't just some suggestion; it's a non-negotiable, a fundamental truth you need to engrave on your soul right now.

Rule #1: You deserve to live an epic, delicious, passionate and loving life being authentically YOU.

Yeah, I said it. You don't have to be some celebrity who gets paid millions to share glimpses of your life, or a "nepo baby" born into fame and fortune. You, just as you are right now, with all your quirks and your messiness and your magnificent potential – YOU deserve that life.

Think about it: nobody else on this entire planet has your DNA. Nobody has your particular history, your past lives (if you believe in that), or your life experiences. You are a one-of-a-kind masterpiece, and it's time you started living like it. Authenticity isn't a luxury; it's your birthright.

The Science Behind Being Your Glorious Self

And this isn't just me spouting mystical wisdom, my little conjuror. Science backs this up! Researchers have been digging into the whole "authenticity" thing, and guess what they've found?

It Boosts Your Well-Being: Studies consistently show that individuals who embrace their true selves report higher levels of happiness, reduced stress, and a more profound sense of life satisfaction. When your actions, beliefs, and values are aligned with who you truly are, your brain literally lights up with feel-good chemicals like serotonin and dopamine! It's like your brain is giving you a high-five for being real.

Better Relationships (Duh): When you're authentic, you build genuine connections. People trust you more. Research has shown that authentic living is linked to better relationships with others and a greater sense of personal growth. Because honestly, who wants to be friends with a walking, talking curated highlight reel all the time?

Increased Resilience: Being authentic actually helps you bounce back from life's inevitable punches. When you know who you are at your core, you're better equipped to manage difficulties and are more resilient during emotional challenges. You're not spending energy pretending, which frees up your mental battery to actually deal with stuff.

Less Mental Health Drama: When you suppress your true self to fit in, you create a massive disconnect between who you are and who you're pretending to be. This "dissonance" can lead to feelings of confusion, emptiness, burnout, and a lack of fulfillment. It's like wearing a ridiculously tight shoe all day – eventually, it's just painful. Studies have linked inauthenticity to higher rates of anxiety, depression, and stress. So, being you isn't just nice, it's a mental health superpower!

How Social Media Distorts Rule #1 (The Sneaky Saboteur)

Now, here's where modern life throws a massive wrench into this beautiful authenticity machine: social media. Oh, that glorious, soul-sucking, comparison-inducing beast. It completely distorts Rule #1 in insidious ways:

The Performance Trap: Social media turns self-expression into a performance. You're not just sharing; you're performing for likes, comments, and shares. This creates a powerful incentive to conform to what's popular or aesthetically pleasing, rather than what feels genuinely resonant to your inner self. You start asking, "What will get more likes?" instead of "What feels true to me?"

The Disappearing Self: When you're constantly adapting your voice, your topics, and even your emotional tone to fit a platform's culture, you can start to fragment your own identity. You develop an "online persona" that diverges from your offline reality. This disconnect can lead to feelings of self-alienation and a loss of individuality, making it harder to even know who your true self is anymore. One study even found that for Gen Z, while perceived authenticity on social media did correlate with better mental health, suggesting some young people are actively trying to separate their online performance from their true selves.

Validation Addiction: Those little red notification bubbles? They're pure dopamine hits. Social media trains your brain to seek external validation for your self-worth. If your post doesn't get enough likes, you might delete it, internalizing that lack of external approval as a sign that you aren't good enough. This is the opposite of authentic self-acceptance, which comes from within, not from a double-tap.

"Don't ask what the world needs. Ask what makes you come alive, and go do it. Because what the world needs is people who have come alive."
– Howard Thurman

Stop waiting for permission. Your authentic passion is the missing piece the world's been waiting for.

Rule #2: Nobody is responsible for creating that epic, delicious life but YOU.

Let me say that again for the folks in the back: NOBODY. ELSE. Not your chosen deity, your parents, your spouse, or that perfectly filtered influencer whose reels claim to have all the answers. Not your astrologer, your priest, your rabbi, or your IG sage. They can offer guidance, inspiration, and a good kick in the pants, but the heavy lifting? The actual creation? That's on you, baby.

What's Your Major Definite Purpose?

So you're asking, "Excuse me miss, how do I take responsibility to create this fabulous life"? By finding your purpose. Your sacred mission. Remember when Neo stopped running from Agent Smith in the Matrix? And Morpheus said, he's beginning to believe. Believe what? That he was the one.

Well, guess what superstar? YOU'RE THE ONE. The only one who can do what you came here to do. The only one with your specific brand of genius, your totally unique quirks, and that one-of-a-kind saga of yours.

It's about tapping into that burning "why." That thing that lights you up, even when people question it, when they look at you with a head tilt and ask "really?". That thing that feels like your personal mission, your non-negotiable contribution to the universe. When you find it, it's like plugging into a cosmic power outlet. And once you identify your purpose, then you are tapping into your Super Power.

It's been done since the history of our blessed planet. Magnificent rebels who felt the undeniable calling that felt like it was written in their soul. It's the thing that makes you jump out of bed, ready to tackle obstacles, because you know you're here to do this.

Here are a few folks who didn't just stumble into success; they tuned into that internal radio station broadcasting their unique purpose and then blasted it out to the world. They faced challenges, sure, but their mission was their fuel.

- **Dr. Jane Goodall**. What do you do when chimpanzees are your devotion, but you belong to a starchy Victorian family? Her purpose expanded beyond research to become a global advocate for conservation and animal welfare. She didn't just study chimps; she became their voice. Farewell Jane, I hope you're now reunited with your beloved Gombe family.

- **Temple Grandin**: She used autism to experience the world like cows do. Yes cows. She didn't just empathize with cows; she understood them on a level nobody else did and revolutionized the entire agricultural industry to reduce their stress and suffering.

- **Dr. Rodrigo Medellín** "The Bat Man of Mexico" is a Mexican ecologist who understood bats' vital role in the North American ecosystem. His sacred mission saved the lesser long-nosed bat from extinction, which is crucial for pollinating agave plants. We Tequila lovers salute you, bat man!

These folks refused to conform to the safe, sleepy script or inherit a legacy that didn't fit. Instead, they tapped into the inner roar—that unique blend of their core identity, deepest passions, and potential for world-shaking impact. You don't need a specific title like corporate rebel or eco-advocate. You just need to be absolutely, unapologetically you.

What turns YOU on? Unleash Your Inner Rockstar

Try this at home. Take a minute, find a piece of paper, and divide it right down the middle like you're cutting a cake that's about to change your life.

On the right side, I want you to unleash your inner fangirl/fanboy. Jot down 5 things you absolutely, positively, can't-live-without LOVE to do. We're talking pure joy here. The stuff that makes your heart blow kisses and your soul do a happy dance.

Now, skip over to the left side. This is where you flex those natural superpowers. List 5 things you're naturally, effortlessly, ridiculously GOOD at. Think about what comes so easy to you that you sometimes forget it's a gift. The stuff people always ask you for help with, or that you just get without even trying.

Why are we doing this little artistic masterpiece, you ask? Because when you're zeroing in on your true purpose, you want it to feel like slipping into your favorite, most comfortable jeans. You want it to be effortless. Think about it: Who in their right mind wants to spend their precious days crammed into a tiny cubicle, wrestling with grumpy customers about their laptop meltdowns, when the very thought of talking to people makes you want to ghost work?! Not you, that's who!

Here's what my list looks like.

The "Superpower Finder"
Exercise: Discover Your Purpose

Things I do Naturally	Things I Love to do
1. Walk fast - seriously I move through the streets of NYC like a ninja.	1. Gardening, honestly, I can't live without dirt under my fingernails.
2. Challenging Beliefs: like why can't girls climb trees?	2. Conversating - Yup, talking is my favorite.
3. Finding big patterns in behavior, society, people, events.	3. Running or hiking in nature, even better if a dog is tagging along.
4. Action oriented - I'm always in motion; I can't sit still. I'm writing this book standing up.	4. Companionship - I'm a Sagittarius, I was born to have a partner in crime.
5. Organizing people to achieve a goal - call me the wedding planner for Corp America.	5. Driving - weird but driving gets me into receptive mode. When I'm stalled with a problem I hop into the car and drive!

Finding the Convergence: The "AHA!" Moments

Let's cross-pollinate these bad boys: Where do the two sides meet? How can I use the things I love, to do things naturally?

Action-Oriented + Running/Hiking in Nature: Since I'm always in motion, I love being active outdoors. Potentially I could channel this as an adventure guide, outdoor fitness guru, environmental activist leading expeditions, or even a nature photographer who captures movement and patterns in the wild. My "Ninja Warrior" speed could lead hiking groups through challenging terrains or even be used in competitive nature-based sports. Ahem, aren't I writing a book about Marathons?

Challenging Beliefs + Gardening: This is real life for me! Not just pie in the sky. I'm taking my passion for gardening and using it to build a foundation that sponsors inner-city kids to visit outdoor spaces. Teaching them how to plant flowers and veggies, how to nurture nature, the value of growing and eating healthy foods. Most importantly, how to get their hands gloriously dirty!

See how it works?

Real Life Example: Nadege

Let me tell you about one of my favorite success stories, my client Nadege, name changed to protect her fabulousness. She worked in a global management consultancy but was languishing. Like a beautiful houseplant left in the dark, she was fading. Why? Because she felt totally disconnected from her purpose. So, the big question was: How do we reinvent her? How do we shift this corporate powerhouse into something that sets her soul on fire?

Guess what we unearthed as her absolute, undeniable passion? Teaching kids how to leverage math to create meaningful and lucrative careers! But not just any math — math as a tool for their dreams. She didn't just think about it, either. Nadege quit her job, opened a math franchise, and is now absolutely rocking her own business with over 200 students. She's transformed herself into a powerhouse speaker, educator, and entrepreneur who's making academic achievement accessible to all kids.

The Convergence Factor: Where Your Genius Explodes!

Now let's get to YOUR Convergence Factor.

Think of it this way: your **natural abilities** are the perfectly tuned engine under your hood—powerful, efficient, and uniquely yours. Your **passions** are the high-octane fuel that makes that engine truly roar. When you bring these two forces together, you don't just drive; you launch into orbit!

This isn't a complex spreadsheet formula (because your purpose is too epic for mere numbers!), but a dynamic equation for insight and unstoppable action.

The Formula for Unlocking Your Edge

Here's how to "calculate" your personal Convergence Factor:

> Convergence Factor=Optimal Application of (Natural Talent) + Deep Engagement with (Passionate Love)

How to Find Your Intersection

To "calculate" your personal Convergence Factor, you just need to connect the dots between your instinct and your interest.

How to "Calculate" It:

1. Identify a Core Natural Talent: Pick one from your "Things I Do Naturally" list.

2. Identify a Core Love: Pick one from your "Things I Love to Do" list.

3. Brainstorm the Intersection: How can you use that talent within or through that love? Ask yourself the high-leverage questions that link these two, forcing your genius to converge:

   - "How can my Natural Talent make Passionate Love more impactful, innovative, or exciting?"

     Example: How can my ability to Simplify Complexity make Mentoring Young Professionals more effective? Answer: By creating easy-to-use career roadmaps.

- "What kind of work or project would allow me to fully express my Natural Talent while being completely immersed in Passionate Love?"

  Example: Designing a visual guide or a step-by-step masterclass that breaks down intimidating industry jargon into simple, digestible steps.

- "Who needs my Natural Talent applied to their Passionate Love-related problems?"

  Example: HR departments looking to onboard recent college graduates, or non-profits that need to translate dense industry regulations into accessible training materials for new staff.

Experiment, test and research: The calculation isn't a one-time thing; it's an ongoing process of investigation and unfolding. Take small steps, volunteer, start a side project, or just talk to people doing things that combine these elements. Research areas, roles, industries that could use your skills. Look into niches that offer the amenities and lifestyle you seek. Explore people who are using their purpose in ways that incentivize you. Your "Convergence Factor" isn't a static number; it's the ever-evolving sweet spot where your authentic self meets your most fulfilling work.

Also, do a gut check. Which convergence point on your list really makes your heart thump? Chase that one!

Tools for Your Blockbuster Life: The Marathon Mindset

By now, I can practically hear your brain buzzing with a question: "So wait a minute! Are you telling me runners are less negative AND have better lives than the rest of us mere mortals?"

Not necessarily, you magnificent skeptic!

Here's the absolute truth bomb: They've mastered the hardcore techniques that obliterate that negativity programming we've **all** been shackled with. They don't just hope for a better life; they know exactly how to engineer the mind, body, and spirit to crank out the results they truly desire.

This isn't some magic pill, nor is it a one-time ceremony. It's about showing up, doing the gritty work. It's about identifying those obnoxious obstacles that are hogging the road to your dreams, then kicking them to the curb. It's about facing your fears head-on, because that's where the real transformation happens.

There's an Oprah Winfrey quote I absolutely live by: "Tell me your worst fear, and I'll show you your next lesson."

So, are you ready to learn? Are you ready to stop letting that inner critic run the show and start living the blockbuster life you were always meant to have?

Your Brain – Your Very Own Supercomputer

This isn't just a book of lessons, case studies, and exercises. Oh no, this is a completely new program designed to revolutionize your inner world. But here's the kicker: You have to choose to download and run it.

Why? Because we're tapping into your brain's magnificent superpower: **Neuroplasticity.** This is your brain's incredible ability to rewire, reshape, and even grow new cells throughout your entire life. Think of your brain as your very own, personal **supercomputer**, capable of anything you program it to do. If there was a magic pill to unleash your potential, you'd take it, right? If there was an "Easy" button for peace of mind, you'd push it, right?

Well, this program is that pill, that button. We're talking about the brain-bending magic of running and how it literally rewires your noggin for peace, purpose, and pure joy. It's not just about getting sweaty; it's about transforming your brain into a five-star resort! The strategies in this program are its ultimate upgrade.

Lacing up your sneakers doesn't just activate your glutes—it unleashes a powerful, purposeful chemical upgrade on your brain. Here's how you dynamically rewire your mental landscape:

The "Good Vibes" Chemical Cocktail: Forget the old-school idea that endorphins are the only thing making you feel good. Running triggers a cocktail of feel-good compounds, including endocannabinoids, which are your body's own natural bliss compounds. They rapidly cross the blood-brain barrier to reduce anxiety and instantly create that feeling of calm euphoria. We'll dive into the full chemistry of joy in Chapter 4!

BDNF: Your Brain's Fertilizer: Running stimulates the production of Brain-Derived Neurotrophic Factor (BDNF). Think of BDNF as a super-charged fertilizer for your brain cells. It supports the survival of existing neurons, promotes the growth of new ones (a process called neurogenesis, especially in the hippocampus – more on that in a sec!), and strengthens the connections between them. Higher levels of BDNF are directly linked to improved cognitive function, better mood, and increased resilience to stress. It literally makes your brain healthier and more adaptable.

Growing New Brain Cells (Hello, Hippocampus!): This is where it gets seriously cool. Consistent aerobic activity promotes neurogenesis in the hippocampus. This region is crucial for memory, learning, and emotional regulation. When you grow new cells here and strengthen those connections, you're building a more robust, efficient brain. This enhanced brain function helps you process emotions better, think more clearly, and ultimately, feel more grounded and purposeful. It's like adding new, high-speed lanes to your brain's highway system!

Rewiring for Resilience (Stress Response Reset): Running puts a healthy, manageable stress on your body. This "good" stress actually trains your brain's stress response system to become more efficient. Over time, regular running helps reduce the levels of stress hormones like cortisol and strengthens your brain's ability to cope with everyday challenges. Your brain learns to differentiate between a physical exertion and a true threat, making you less reactive and more resilient to life's curveballs. You become a mental warrior, able to glide through stressful situations.

The Meditative Loop and Clarity: The repetitive, rhythmic nature of running can act as a form of moving meditation. Focusing on your breath, your steps, and the environment around you can quiet the incessant chatter in your mind. This "digital detox" allows for mental clarity, sharper focus, and helps you break free from cycles of negative thinking. When your mind is clear and calm, it's so much easier to tap into what truly matters to you, to identify your values, and to align with your purpose.

So, when you hit the pavement, you're not just exercising your body; you're actively, dynamically, and powerfully rewiring your brain. You're building a stronger, calmer, more adaptable mental landscape that makes peace, purpose, and productivity not just fleeting desires, but tangible realities.

Pssst: get the upgrade, it's free.

From Pavement to Power Suit

Listen up, all you non-runners out there! This works for everyone. Not just race enthusiasts.

"Marathon Mindset" – rooted in running techniques and the incredible power of neuroplasticity isn't just about feeling good; it's about getting tangibly better at every aspect of your professional life, whether you're climbing the corporate ladder, saving lives in medicine, shaping young minds in education, mastering a trade, or conquering your studies as a student.

Think of it like this: your career is a marathon, not a sprint. It's got long stretches of grind, unexpected hills, moments where you hit a wall, and times you need to surge. The "Marathon Mindset" gives you the internal operating system to dominate it all.

Here's how running techniques and neuroplasticity provide concrete advantages in the business arena.

Your Brain's Competitive Edge

1. Peak Performance & Focus:

Running's disciplined focus on breath and pace literally rewires your prefrontal cortex. You stop getting derailed by every notification, every *look squirrel!* that distracts you. This mental clarity is your competitive edge, giving you the ability to make sound decisions under pressure and maintain laser focus during complex tasks.

2. Superior Stress Management:

Running controls panic. The "runner's high" is your body flooding itself with natural chill pills while suppressing cortisol. The result? You become Teflon in the office. You handle criticism with composure because your brain has learned the difference between a real threat and a Tuesday afternoon email storm.

3. Creative Problem Solving:

The rhythmic motion frees your mind to wander and solve problems, spiking your brain's fertilizer. Innovative solutions find you because your brain is connecting dots the overstressed competition can't even see.

The "Marathon Mindset" isn't just a metaphor; it's a practical, neurologically-backed framework for cultivating the mental toughness, clarity, and emotional mastery required to excel in today's demanding business landscape. It's a choice you make to transform your brain into your friend, your alley, and the ultimate tool for success.

Don't Diss the Elixir

My husband is a Chiropractor and Acupuncturist. He has a doctorate in herbal medicine, so he's fascinated by herbal remedies that bring the body into stasis, and into health. We take a ton of supplements, to keep our bodies pain-free, maintain healthy systems, muscle, bone, digestion, you name it!

So when our friend lamented, "Oh, my memory's going! I wish I had something to keep my mind alert!" Wayne jumped into attention. referred her to a doctor who could prescribe a specific supplement – a derivative of ginseng to keep her brain sharp and clear. Basically, like she's thirty-three again. We checked in with her a few weeks later, eager to hear about her newfound mental superpowers.

Her reply? "No, I just can't get into the habit of taking it."

I was boggled. Absolutely stunned. You have a magical elixir right there, capable of keeping your brain humming, and you can't get into the habit of taking it?!

Here's the lesson for you, my friend: **Take the damn elixir!**

If you're reading this book, you're already in the elite 5%. You're a soul seeker, a curious thinker, a self-awareness hound! You're hungry for more. So get ready to feast.

Look, mastering a negative mindset is a process, not a magic trick. It takes time and effort. Your brain will keep playing the old program until you give it something else to run. So why not give it a marvelous new script? But here's the unvarnished truth, straight from my lips to your breathtaking brain: There's work involved. A ton of work. And let me be totally frank, it's not always pretty.

So don't you dare get discouraged if you don't see results immediately. You didn't become a master of negative self-talk overnight, and you won't become a Zen master overnight either.

The Fine Print (But Still Awesome)

Be Kind to Yourself. Everybody has negative thoughts from time to time. You're human, not a robot. Don't beat yourself up for having them. Instead, acknowledge them, give them a little nod, and then gently redirect your focus to thoughts that actually serve you.

And here's a big one: Get Help. This book is your kick-ass roadmap, your personal pep talk, your secret weapon. But it is not intended to replace professional medical or mental health help. If you're truly struggling to manage your negative mindset on your own, please, for the love of all that is holy, do not hesitate to seek professional help. The market is absolutely flooded with incredible medical professionals, experts, coaches who use innovative and time-tested techniques to be your ultimate cheerleader and help reprogram your mind into one that is safe, supportive, and ready to kick ass.

Think about it: How can you be a truly great leader when you're not a great person first? You can't. It takes dedication and commitment to do the work. Period.

And no, you absolutely, positively do NOT have to be a marathoner or some hardcore distance runner to snag all the insane benefits from this book! While those long-distance heroes have some serious, mind-blowing secrets tucked away in their running shoes, the fundamental principles apply to every single one of us.

I've been lucky to coach and work with people from all five generations on this stuff. We're talking wide-eyed Gen Zers with dreams as big as the sky, navigating their first big leaps. We're talking wisdom-filled members of the Silent Generation (aka Traditionalists). We're talking Baby Boomers and Gen Xers, who thought they'd seen it all. And now, I'm even diving in with the Alphas!

I've seen the Marathon Mindset transform:

Performance Leadership	**Performance Psychology**	**Performance Training**
Fortune 500. Leadership. C-Suite. Leadership Legacy. ROI Focus. Management. Personal Transformation. Professional Development.	Mental Fortitude. Imposter Syndrome. Elite Performance. Rewiring Patterns & Behavior. Fears & Phobias. Strategic Resilience. Boundary Setting.	Goal Setting. 26.2 Miles. Endurance Techniques. Visualization. Mental Rehearsal. Neurobiology. Recovery Mastery.

Epiphany Turned into Practice: Your Life, Your Masterpiece

It's been four decades since my teenage epiphany. Four decades! And I can tell you, hand on my heart: I am living the life I always dreamed. I've become the person I always wanted to be.

I've had mind-blowing success teaching these principles everywhere from the high-stakes trading floors of Financial Services to the client-obsessed showrooms of Luxury Automotive, and deep inside the innovation hubs of global Technology firms. And for all the negative press Gen Z sometimes gets, I was absolutely delighted to see how they devoured these principles in the two-day workshops I conducted. They're hungry for real tools!

Why do these ideas work everywhere? Because the core traits of high performers are universal. Vana Hutter, a legit expert on athletic mental health, discovered that top athletic performers possess off-the-charts levels of self-confidence, dedication, and focus, plus the uncanny ability to concentrate and handle pressure like a boss.

Sound uncannily similar to the traits of a high-performing Leader? There's a reason for that. Highly developed Leaders are people who unapologetically invest in themselves. Not just in their professional skills, but, crucially, in their personal operating system. They know that peak performance is a holistic pursuit.

The Grim Question, My Awesome Answer

But you ask, isn't all this good vibes stuff awfully Mary Tyler Moore? Like unicorns and rainbows, and flinging your hat in the air?

Maybe. Maybe it's got a dash of that wholesome optimism. But guess what? We're not just talking about being vaguely nice or the occasional smile; we're talking about actively forging a whole new way to be human. A happier, more resilient, utterly unstoppable human. A human who's not just existing, but living their purpose and absolutely exploding with fulfillment.

But shouldn't I be tough and a badass? You might counter. Aren't I supposed to win and succeed at life?

YES! Absolutely! You should be tough, you should be a conqueror, and you should absolutely win and succeed at life! But do you have to be an asshole while doing it?! Seriously. Because if you come back in the next life as a paramecium, don't you dare bitch at me.

You can be kind and crush it. You can be empathetic and unstoppable. You can be compassionate and a total powerhouse. It's not either/or, darling. It's both. And frankly, the "both" version is way more fun and gets you way further in the long run.

So get ready.

To create your own blockbuster movie, to manifest the reality you dream about, it all starts with two foundational, non-negotiable principles:

1. It's your birthright to an epic life. You were made for this.
2. Nobody can create it but YOU. You're the hero, the director, the star.

Committed to making your movie a blockbuster? Ready to unleash the unstoppable force that is YOU? Let's look at the factors that prevent you from not only living the life of your dreams, but keep you locked in the same patterns and behaviors.

Rules of Road

Here's your Finisher medal for reviewing the movie of your life.

- You learned the 2 commandments for creating a Marathon Mindset.

- Are you ready to embrace your authenticity and responsibility?

- You aced the Super Power Finder Quiz.

- Now are you excited about your Convergence Factor where you genius explodes?

- Don't you love how runners use neuroplasticity to create a good vibes cocktail? Bring on the BDNF!

- The big reveal–the Marathon Mindset works for everyone. Not just race enthusiasts.

- You discovered that the core traits of high performers are universal: self-confidence, dedication, and focus, plus the uncanny ability to concentrate and handle pressure like a boss.

Ready to unearth why all of us are wired for negativity?

CHAPTER 2

WHAT IF NEGATIVITY WAS A DEFAULT, NOT YOUR FAULT?

Tell me something. How do you start your day? Seriously, what's the first thing you do when you crack open those sleepy eyelids? You can tell me.

Do you lay there feeling bewildered, waiting for your brain to click into ON mode, and then get hit by a tsunami of thoughts?

- That monster deadline for the pitch is TODAY?!

- Did I hit 'send' on that email, or is it still sitting in drafts haunting my soul?!

- Crap, we're out of cereal and now the kids are going to mutiny like sugar-deprived pirates!

Sound familiar?

Then, naturally, your hand gravitates to your phone, because, of course, it's charging right next to your head. You scroll through the calendar, check your texts, and then — BAM! — you see a notification for a miracle green salt that melts pounds away while you sleep, and also gives you unicorn powers. Despite your urgent meeting, you're totally intrigued and click on that shimmering, ridiculous salt bait. Which, naturally, catapults you straight into the Instagram abyss, where a mazelike selection of digital goodies is served up to you. Puppies in tiny, knitted hats that look like they're about to drop a mixtape. An outraged video about what you absolutely, positively won't believe happens at 4:35. (Spoiler: probably nothing). Kittens delivering lightning-fast slaps to bewildered human faces. Recipes for cauliflower pancakes that taste suspiciously like regret. And, of course, a "coach" who promises to make you six figures before the week is over, just by thinking really, really hard.

Don't feel bad, my little dreamer. That's how almost everybody wakes up these days. But I'm here to show you something new. It all starts with that first conscious breath. Are you ready to rewrite the opening scene of your day?

Your Quantum Wake-Up Call

How about we try it a little differently?

You awaken. Sleep has utterly wiped the slate of your thoughts clean. And for one miraculous, fleeting moment, anything – and I mean anything – is possible. That, my friend, is your Quantum Potential just waiting for you to tap in! Think of it this way: it's that split second before your brain's usual programming kicks in, where every single possibility, every single choice for your day, for your life, is simultaneously vibrating with pure, unadulterated potential. It's the blank canvas of infinite possibility!

Instead of letting your mind race like a Derby contender, you take a glorious, slow breath. You fill your lungs with that fresh, new day energy. And then, you utter these newfound truths to yourself:

> *"Every day I become a better me. Peace is my compass. Joy is my birthright."*

You wiggle those toes. Your knees, your head – give 'em a little stretch. You feel the mattress cushioning your body, cradling you in comfort. You snuggle into that pillow for just one more, delicious moment. You take a deep, soul-cleansing breath and you give yourself a secret smile. You've got another fresh 24 hours to be your best self.

You think of all the sweet rewards: "I'm grateful for a beautiful night of deep sleep. For the excellent dinner we devoured last night. For the pure fun we had watching the kids crush it at their game."

Then, you set yourself up for a new day: Today, I am creating another scene from the movie of my life. It's going to roll smoothly. I've already invested in all the hard work – the heartache, the overtime, the tears, the grit. All I have to do is simply feel like the absolute best version of myself. Because I've invested in becoming a force of nature, a magnet for miracles, an honorable human, the universe is about to reward me in ways I can't even begin to imagine.

You stretch, you rub your beloved on the tush, hear them mumble appreciatively, and roll out of bed.

Rewriting Your Inner Script: From Panic to Power

You don't even realize it, but your mind has been programmed, practically hard-wired, to wake up to panic. You see, it's been meticulously trained from years of pattern-driven behavior – patterns you might not even be consciously aware of, patterns that have been embedded into you for thousands of years. Thank your ancestors for the survival instincts, but a little less daily dread would be nice!

If the personal movie of your life isn't the blockbuster you envisioned, it's high time to change the script. This means actively swapping out the default you've been running on, probably since forever. The monumental significance of this? It's simple: once you truly grasp that your day, your *entire reality*, can unfold exactly the way you want, you've unequivocally accepted the power to direct it.

Why do we accept the panic loop? Because our minds are programmed to chase the familiar—what's easy, what's Known. Your brain associates the Known with Safety, even if the familiar means you're muttering, "I'm sick of feeling like panic is my ride-along best friend." We are miserably, intimately familiar with fear, and that familiarity is what we keep chasing, even when it leads straight into the dark forest.

So, here's the game-changer: What if there was a different setting? What if happiness was your default—your everyday, automatic state? Wouldn't that be the ultimate script twist?

Really Good Questions to Ask #1: Your Personal GPS to Breakthrough

Let's get down to brass tacks. Over the years, I've developed some seriously killer hacks for dismantling those pesky feelings, beliefs, and situations that just didn't sit right with my soul. Remember how I mentioned my natural-born superpower for challenging beliefs? Yeah, well, it comes in handy when I hit those inevitable brick walls.

You know the feeling: you're pushing, you're grinding, you're practically banging your head against what feels like an impenetrable barrier. You're stuck, frustrated, and ready to throw your hands up in the air and declare yourself a card-carrying member of the resignation club. That's precisely when I whip out my secret weapon, the question that has literally rerouted my entire trajectory.

When I hit that wall, when the old ways just aren't cutting it, I stop, take a breath, and ask the universe (or my subconscious, or whatever magical force is listening):

"Can you show me a better way to do this?

It sounds simple, right? Almost too simple. But don't let its minimal phrasing fool you. This isn't just a question; it's a declaration of intent. It's you, consciously, emphatically, telling the universe: "I'm open. I'm ready for a different solution. I'm humbling myself to higher wisdom, because my answers stink."

Because when you ask this question with genuine openness, you're not just whining about your problem. You're commanding your brain to shift gears. You're essentially sending out a cosmic flare, signaling that you're ready to receive guidance, new strategies, and fresh perspectives you might not even know exist.

So, the next time you feel that familiar thud against the wall, don't just stand there feeling defeated. Instead, take a breath, straighten your crown, and ask with unwavering conviction: "Can you show me a better way to do this?"

Watch what happens next. The answers might not come in a puff of smoke, but they'll come.

Your Brain: The Ancient Alarm System

Let's yank back the curtain and unravel the glorious, messy truth about how your magnificent brain got wired the way it is. You deserve to know, and you absolutely deserve to understand why none of us — not even the Zen masters — are immune to its ancient quirks.

> *"Your Mind is Velcro for Negativity and Teflon for Good." Rick Hanson, author of Rewiring Happiness*

Your Brain Is Wired to Protect (Seriously, It's Obsessed)

It's taken humans hundreds of thousands of years to evolve into the creatures we are today. And this evolution? It's been driven by the glacial pace of genetic mutation, brutal natural selection, and our bodies desperately adapting to a world of constant environmental drama. The result? We're all walking around with an ancient, threat-averse brain, honed for pure survival in a world of scarcity and immediate, tooth-and-claw physical dangers. Yes, even you, chilling in your comfy chair in an age of unparalleled tech.

Let's talk about this brain of yours, this magnificent three-pound universe we carry around. If you've spent any time being human, you've probably noticed it's got this... well, this tendency towards the gloomy. And there's an ancient, really good reason for that, rooted in our very survival, way back when we were dodging sabretooth tigers and figuring out which berries wouldn't kill us.

Our brains evolved in an environment where every rustle in the bushes could be a predator, every unfamiliar face a potential threat. Missing a threat, even once, could be fatal. So, our ancestors with brains that were hyper-vigilant, that quickly spotted danger and remembered it vividly – they were the ones who lived to pass on their genes. That's you and me, folks. We're the proud, slightly anxious descendants of the worrywarts, the ones who jumped at shadows and survived to tell the tale.

And, let's face it, our brains are still obsessed with threats more than opportunities. It's not a flaw, not exactly. It's a deeply ingrained survival mechanism, a relic from a time when being hyper-vigilant to danger was the literal difference between life and death. Your brain's primary directive is to keep you safe, and it does that by paying more attention to what could hurt you.

Your Brain Is a Pattern-Finding Genius (Especially for the Bad Stuff!)

Your brain is absolutely fabulous at finding patterns. Superpower! Unfortunately, in ancient times, it primarily focused on negative patterns because a happy sing-along by the fire, while warming, wasn't what kept people alive through a freezing winter or a famine.

In a world where missing a real threat could mean death, it was actually safer to see a pattern where none existed. Think about it: a rustle might just be the wind, but your ancestor who thought "predator!" and ran, survived. The one who thought "just the wind" became lunch. So, our brains are wired to prioritize finding negative patterns. It's a legacy of our evolutionary past, a system that kept us alive in a dangerous world. Your brain is just trying to keep you safe. That's its job!

The Glitch in Your Genius: The Negativity Bias Exposed

This ancient wiring created what we now call negativity bias. Here's a perfect example: Imagine you're hiking in the woods with friends. You're soaking in the symphony of birds, admiring trees heavy with lush leaves, breathing in the fresh scent of pine. While enjoying the scenery, you suddenly spot a rattlesnake! It immediately slithers away, no harm done. However, when asked about the hike later, what's the most vivid memory? You got it: the rattlesnake incident sticks with you way more than the beautiful scenery.

Your Inner Witch Doctor

I can guarantee almost every single one of us harbors at least one mildly superstitious behavior. And guess what? That's totally okay! It stems directly from your negativity bias working overtime, trying to make sense of a world that, for our ancestors, was basically one giant, unpredictable death trap.

Imagine trying to navigate life without antibiotics, without weather apps, without Gemini to tell you why your cow just dropped dead. Every weird occurrence, every sniffle, every bad harvest? It had to be something. And that's where the truly bananas superstitions came in. They weren't just quirky habits; they were sophisticated (if misguided) survival strategies for a brain convinced everything was out to get it.

You might not be sacrificing goats or wearing dried toad parts like our medieval ancestors (Goat Yoga, thanks you). But don't think for a second that we're somehow immune to the pull of superstition in our "enlightened" modern world! That ancient brain wiring is still humming along, trying to find patterns, trying to exert control, and still absolutely terrified of bad stuff happening. So, even if you roll your eyes at the idea of a crystal ball, check this out:

Black Cats: From Witch's Familiar to Plague Buster

Let's bust this ridiculous superstition right now! For centuries, the sight of a sleek, beautiful black cat crossing your path has been seen by many as an omen of doom. But where did that terrifying notion come from?

Well, brace yourself for some medieval madness. In the 13th century, Pope Gregory IX dropped a bombshell, issuing a document called "Vox in Rama" that explicitly linked black cats to Satan himself. Talk about a smear campaign! This fueled rampant fear and persecution, turning these innocent felines into scapegoats. Black cats quickly became synonymous with witches' "familiars" – supernatural sidekicks believed to assist them in their dark magic.

This utterly bonkers belief led to black cats often being captured and brutally killed alongside accused witches during the Inquisitions and witch hunts throughout Europe. And here's the ultimate twist of cruel irony: this mass slaughter of cats actually contributed to the spread of the devastating Bubonic Plague. With their primary predators wiped out, rodent populations exploded, carrying the plague-infested fleas far and wide.

So, the next time a black kitty saunters across your path, remember its true history. It's not a bringer of bad luck; it's a survivor of terrible human ignorance, and arguably, a heroic, albeit misunderstood, plague fighter!

Witch Hunts: When Fear Becomes the Operating System

The persecution of women as witches is directly tied to the paranoia surrounding the "familiar" and the power of fear.

This wasn't about magic; it was about toxic default settings—namely, fear, social control, and deep-seated misogyny during times of intense hardship.

- The Misogyny Playbook: The Church, via texts like the Malleus Maleficarum, provided the rigid doctrine, declaring women morally weaker and ripe for the Devil's picking.

- The Scapegoat Strategy: In a world without science, when crops failed or a baby died, society needed an immediate answer. It was easier to blame a defenseless neighbor—often a midwife, healer, widow, or spinster—than to admit to poor hygiene or bad luck.

This persecution was the ultimate act of social terror, fueled by the terrifying, baseless idea that women were making a pact with the Devil. The trials were used to brutally enforce conformity and punish any woman who stepped outside the narrow lines of acceptable behavior.

This is what happens when fear, rather than logic, becomes the operating system. It's the purest example of the human tendency to embrace the Negativity Default.

Your Brain's Overdue Upgrade

Do you now see why negativity is a human Default, not your actual Fault? Paying attention to the negative kept us alive. If given the choice, we would all choose happiness, pleasure and sweet sensations. Gone are the sabretooth tigers; matter of fact, almost all the tigers are gone! We don't live in prairies or jungles where we can become lunch. But our brain, bless its overprotective heart, doesn't know this and keeps us in a holding pattern, a survival plot that no longer serves us.

The Slow Burn: Why Evolution Isn't a Race

And I'm not just talking about the slow-motion, Neanderthal-to-modern-human kind of evolution. I'm talking about the massive shifts between entire eras. It took humans thousands of years to transform from hunter-gatherers to the Agrarian era, with its farming and domesticated livestock. Then, in a seemingly explosive two hundred years, we practically darted into the Industrial Age, trading farms for factories. Suddenly, specialized knowledge and training for operating industrial production became the hot new skill. This even opened doors for women and children to work outside the home, adding crucial income. Manufacturing, steel, automotives, petroleum, trains, automation, machines like mills and the steam engine – all contributed to this massive Industrial Revolution.

And then, once again, in a blink of an eye in evolutionary terms, we shifted again. From Industrial to Technological. Remember the Renaissance? Guess what? We're living in the Digital Renaissance. The latter 20th Century saw this insane explosion of advancement: computers, digital music, cable television, the internet, the cloud, social media, and most recently, AI. Think about it: almost every human over the age of five now carries a handheld supercomputer cleverly disguised as a phone.

But here's where things get really wild, and it explains so much of the modern angst we're feeling.

Humanity vs. Technology: A Mismatched Race

We've got these two titanic forces at play: human evolution and technological evolution. And guess what? They operate on vastly different timelines. It's like comparing a tortoise to a cheetah. While human evolution is glacial, technology is advancing faster than you can say "software update."

The good news, the really good news, is that understanding this ancient wiring gives us the power to work with our brains, to intentionally cultivate more positive experiences and slowly, gently, rewire those old negativity circuits.

Training your brain away from gloom is like learning to play the piano. The 'old dog' wants to play the same rusty, minor chord every time (the automatic negative thought). To teach it a new trick, you must practice a new, major chord slowly and deliberately. The first dozen times, you have to think about every finger position. But with consistent, patient practice, that new, harmonic chord becomes muscle memory—your default setting— and the 'old trick' fades into a song you haven't played in years.

The Mindset Archetype Quiz: Where Does Your Mental Negativity Stand?

Ready to discover the hidden gears turning in your mind? I've created a fun quiz to uncover your dominant mindset archetype! Let's find out where you stand on the continuum of negativity. Are you little miss sunshine or a prisoner of your mind?

This quiz isn't about judgment; it's designed to offer some wildly insightful clarity into your current relationship with those sneaky negative thoughts and feelings. For each question, choose the answer that resonates most deeply with you. And remember: be honest with yourself – there are no right or wrong answers, just your truth!

Instructions: Choose the answer that resonates most with you for each question. Tally up your letters at the end to reveal your amazing archetype!

Archetype Mindset Quiz

Ready to discover your dominant mindset archetype?Z Let's find out where you stand on the continuum of negativity. Are you little miss sunshine or a prisoner of your mind? Choose the answer that resonates most with you.

1. **You're staring down a challenging project at work that requires you to problem-solve with Al. What's the very first thought that explodes in your brain?**

   a). Whoa! I'm an Al newbie, but bring it on! I'm drooling at the chance to learn this technology.

   b). Cue the stress music. What a nightmare. What if Al takes over my identity? What if I face-plant?

   c). I've got this! I'll break it down into bite-sized chunks like a strategic genius. Al - my new buddy.

   d). Ugh, me? For this? I don't even like Al. Maybe I should just fake a sudden illness.

2. **Someone throws some "constructive criticism" your way. How do you really react?**

a). Yes. Thanks for the awesome feedback! I'm always here for an opportunity to level up.

b). Ouch, that stings like a bee with a tiny grudge. But they're right, because I'm definitely flawed.

c). Interesting. I'll dissect this feedback like a master chef to figure how to turn it into my secret sauce.

d). Clearly they don't know what they're talking about. They don't get the complex picture of my brilliance.

3. **You're trying to conquer a brand-new skill. What's your battle plan?**

a). I'm going to embrace the messy learning process and soak up every moment of this wild journey.

b). I better get good at this, like, pronto. I can't look like a total beginner!

c). I'll hunt down the best resources, drill it into my brain, and practice until I've officially mastered it.

d). I'm pretty sure I was born without the gene for this. Maybe I should just binge-watch Netflix instead.

4. **You hit a major setback. What's your immediate, gut-level response?**

a). Bummer, but guess what? I'll learn from this, shake it off, and keep storming forward!

b). See?! This is exactly what I was afraid of! I knew deep down I was destined to fail.

c). Detective hat time! What went wrong here? How can I tweak my strategy and come back stronger?

d). Seriously? I'm just not cut out for this grand adventure. Time to retreat back to my comfort zone.

5. **You're surrounded by people crushing it, better than you. How does that make you feel?**

a). Inspired, baby! Their success is like rocket fuel for my own goals. Let's go!

b). Honestly? I feel intimidated and inadequate. I'll never be as good as them, so why even try?

c). They're like living, breathing role models, and I'm here to absorb all their wisdom.

d). Ugh, I'm a giant ball of jealousy. It's just not fair. They probably had some secret advantage anyway.

Your Mindset Archetype: Revealed!

Mostly A's: The Growth Mindset Guru

You, my friend, are a force of nature! You practically high-five challenges, see failures as epic opportunities to level up, and know deep down that effort and learning are your superpowers. Your brain is a master of rewriting old, unhelpful patterns, actively seeking new neural pathways. You effortlessly sidestep those negativity bias cues, choosing optimism and resilience instead. Keep shining!

Mostly B's: The Fixed Mindset Friend

Hey there, cozy comfort-seeker! You tend to sidestep challenges and see failure as a personal affront. You might secretly (or not so secretly) believe your abilities are carved in stone, leading to a tango with self-doubt. Your brain is quite comfortable in its pattern-driven behavior, often falling back on what's familiar, even if it's limiting. You're also highly attuned to negativity bias cues, which can reinforce your belief that you're not capable. But here's the secret: your brain is a marvel of neuroplasticity! You absolutely can learn and grow beyond these limits!

Mostly C's: The Strategic Mindset Master

You, brilliant one, are an analytical powerhouse, a goal-oriented tactical genius! You live for planning, dissecting problems, and executing strategies with laser-like focus to achieve epic results. You're adept at identifying and managing negative patterns before they take root, and you use your keen observation skills to recognize and neutralize negativity bias cues that might derail your progress. Continuous improvement isn't just a buzzword for you; it's your way of life.

Mostly D's: The Limiting Mindset Learner

Oh, my sweet, underestimated potential! You often underestimate your own incredible abilities, wrestle with self-confidence, and might be holding yourself back from true greatness. Your brain is deeply entrenched in pattern-driven behavior that reinforces self-doubt, and you're particularly susceptible to negativity bias cues, which can easily convince you to play small. But here's the exhilarating truth: you are bursting with untapped potential, just waiting to be unleashed! This is your moment to break free and soar!

Important Note:

This quiz is just for fun and designed to spark some juicy self-awareness! It's definitely not a definitive psychological assessment. Remember, mindsets are fluid, ever-changing, and totally within your power to sculpt. No matter your archetype today, you hold the keys to cultivating a powerhouse growth mindset and achieving every single magnificent potential you possess!

My Tech Saga: From Typewriters to TikTok

Picture this: I was a wide-eyed sophomore in high school, back in the thrilling year of 1980. Our Pastor's wife, Mrs. Dolores Londis (what a patient soul!), took it upon herself to teach all the girls in the class how to type. And not on some fancy screen, oh no. We learned on a manual typewriter. Yes, you heard me right, the "relic of a bygone era" was, believe it or not, the absolute cutting-edge tech of the day!

This mechanical marvel practically forced a certain kind of discipline. There was no "delete and pretend it never happened" button; every single keystroke was a commitment. Manual typewriters were the gritty workhorses of newsrooms, the confidantes of novelists pouring out their souls, and the literal backbone of offices for decades. They embodied a tangible, beautiful connection to the craft of writing and stand as a charming, clickity-clack reminder of just how far technology has rocketed, and maybe, just maybe, what raw, focused grit we might have lost in the process of gaining all that glossy efficiency.

I devoured that typing skill and used it to Temp. Before "extravagantly paid consultant" was even a twinkle in anyone's eye, there were Temps! Glorious, flexible, incredibly useful Temps. I actually put myself through college by temping during the summers in sweltering Washington, D.C.

I'd hitch a ride with my parents and dive headfirst into temporary gigs at places like the powerhouse Pepco (Potomac Electric Power Company), or at the glitzy, infamous lobbying firms lining K Street. It was my first taste of real-world hustle, all thanks to those strong typing fingers.

Then, when I graduated and made the leap to New York City, I landed at Doubleday Publishing. And let me tell you, that's where I was first introduced to the legendary floppy disk. Oh, the drama! You had to carefully insert it, then meticulously type code into the DOS prompt just to get what would eventually become our beloved MS Office programs to even think about running. It felt like witchcraft, but the kind that got the job done.

When I then shifted gears to Financial Services in the roaring 1990s at Lehman Brothers (remember them?), I practically had a front-row seat to the dizzying arrival of the Internet and Email. I'd have these Managing Directors, hotshots making more money than God, squinting at me and asking, "My kid says I should learn this 'Internet thing.' What can it possibly do for me?" And my answer, with the kind of confidence only an upstart can convey: "Lead generation, gentlemen." Little did they know, it was just the beginning of the digital revolution.

Fast forward to the 2000s when I moved to AIG, and suddenly, social media erupted onto the scene. Again, senior management would scratch their heads, fearing it like it was some ancient Sumerian text: "What can that do for the business?" My answer, with a flourish: "Word-of-mouth marketing. It's like advertising, but 90% more effective, and waaay cheaper."

You know, one of my absolute favorite workshops to conduct is all about how every generation has been uniquely wired, molded, and totally transformed by the technology of its day. And since we're diving deep into the tech-brain connection, here's a quick rundown of how technology has impacted and shaped each generation.

How Tech Wired Your Brain (Gen by Gen!)

So, you're struggling to put down the phone and focus on the deep, difficult work of the Marathon Mindset because your brain has been punked. The struggle to focus isn't a simple failure of willpower; it's a sophisticated consequence of living in a world optimized for instant, frictionless pleasure.

Every device, platform, and algorithm that defined your childhood literally wired your expectations for time, speed, and reward. Let's consider how technology that defined each generation set their internal clock—and why the clock has sped up so drastically.

The Silent Generation (1928–1945)

The Tech: Print media, handwritten letters, radio, black and white TV.

The Wiring: These guys were basically analog machines. News took days, communication was an act of Congress (pen to paper, stamp, mailbox—wait). Their reward was purely institutional: seniority, stability, and the eventual, reliable payoff of decades of quiet conformity. They didn't expect instant answers; they expected eventual, bankable results. This laid a deep foundation for patience and the structural delayed gratification of the long haul. You didn't hit refresh; you waited for the mailman.

Baby Boomers (1946–1964)

The Tech: Color TV, the cable revolution, portable music, early video games (remember Pong?)

The Wiring: Boomers were the first to get the constant flow. Color TV and cable meant the world was more vivid and constantly on. Their internal clock sped up from "institutional time" to "broadcast time." They still had to wait for the 8 PM slot, but they expected pleasure to arrive on schedule and in a giant, televised chunk. The reward shifted to mass cultural payoff—being part of the collective experience. They learned patience, but also the expectation that pleasure, once scheduled, was inevitable.

Generation X (1965–1980)

The Tech: Digital pioneers, the remote control, MTV, VHS/VCR, the home computer, solo gaming.

The Wiring: Gen X was the first generation wired for control and skepticism. The VCR (rewind/fast-forward) and the TV remote gave them unprecedented power to edit reality and choose their own adventure. MTV delivered instant, high-energy visuals. Their reward system was based on self-sufficiency and customization. They learned that information wasn't fixed; it could be manipulated and controlled. This created deep skepticism toward institutions (hence they are known as the "Lost Generation") but also a hard-wired ability to pause and restart—a foundational skill for tackling complex, non-linear work.

Millennials (1981–1996)

The Technology: The internet (dial-up to broadband), email, texting, birth of social media, the iPod.

The Wiring: Millennials were wired for instant information, delayed success. They were the first to experience the "always on" world. Media served up 24/7 news. Email provided instant global communication; Google offered instant answers. Their expectations for access were instant, but their expectations for life rewards (home ownership, career stability) were significantly postponed due to economic realities. This created a high-expectation, low-patience paradox. They learned that effort must be constantly broadcast (early social media), and the reward shifted to the "social-proof" micro-hit—a small, immediate dopamine squirt that validated the self, long before the major payoff materialized.

Generation Z (1997–2012)

The Technology: True digital natives, mobile video (YouTube/TikTok), infinite scroll, personalized algorithms, social media 2.0.

The Wiring: Gen Z is wired for instant dopamine and seamless personalization. They have never known a world without instant news, mobile video, and an algorithm that constantly caters content to their interests. The core technology here is the infinite scroll, which eliminates the mental "stop point" and trains the brain for constant, low-friction consumption. This makes sustained, hard work (which is high-friction and low-reward in the short term) feel frustratingly inefficient. Their reward system demands immediate feedback (the "like") and constant entertainment. The power of postponement is a foreign concept when the brain is used to getting a fresh, tailored hit every 3 seconds.

Generation Alpha (2013–2026)

The Technology: AI (voice assistants), video-centric reality, smart toys, seamless digital/physical reality.

The Wiring: Gen Alpha is being wired for instant interaction and synthetic reality. They are the first generation to grow up with AI as a functional tool, expecting personalized, conversational, and companionship from non-human sources. They live in a world where a physical object (a smart toy) constantly connects to a digital ecosystem, blurring the lines of reality. Their internal clock is optimized for zero friction and conversational access. If they ask a question or want an action, the immediate, personalized response is the reward. For them, any delay—or any interaction that requires sustained physical effort without constant digital assistance—can feel like a technological failure.

Your Turn: What's Your Tech Story?

Alright, now that you've cruised through my tech saga and seen how gadgets shaped entire generations, it's your turn to jump into the hot seat! This isn't just a fun little trip down memory lane; it's a chance to see how the screens, sounds, and connections you grew up with truly wired your brain and shaped who you are today.

Grab a pen, open a new note on your phone, or just noodle on this for a bit. Go on, dive in. Your tech story is uniquely yours, and understanding it is just another key to unlocking your own magnificent brain!

Here's your mission, should you choose to accept it:

- Which magnificent generation do you belong to? (No need to get bogged down in exact years, just pick the one that feels most "you"!). **Insider note**: Since I straddle Boomer and Gen X, that plops me into the micro generation, called Gen Joneser.

- What was the absolute biggest technology that impacted you growing up? Think about the game-changer, the thing that felt like magic or changed how you communicated, learned, or just lived. MTV debuted in 1981. **Insider note**: And I just HAD to have my MTV.

- How did it fundamentally change you? Did it make you more impatient? More connected? More resourceful? Did it open up a whole new world, or maybe even close some doors? Get introspective here. **Insider note**: Parents have always relied on their kids to translate technology.

And for the real soul-searching bonus rounds:

- **Old School or One Click Away**? How did your generation's dominant tech shape how you connected with people? Did you have to actually use a rotary dial to call on a landline (gasp!)? Do you remember waiting for your big sister to stop yakking so you could use it? Were DMs a distant sci-fi fantasy? How did your social life evolve around the tech you had?

- **Information**. Before endless data streams, how did you find out what you needed to know? Did you have to hit the library? Remember microfiche? Was the news Dan Rather at 6:00 pm? Or was information just a quick tap away? What did this lack (or abundance) of instant info do to your brain?

- **Tech Glitch**. What was the most infuriating, yet ultimately character-building, tech challenge your generation faced? Think dial-up sounds, VCR programming nightmares, or perhaps trying to explain a floppy disk to a Gen Z-er!

Every generation was the early adopter of the technology of its day.

There's something to dazzle your noodle. Pretty wild, eh? So don't get all high and mighty just because your teacher can't find the escape button on the smart board.

Score: Technology 999,999, Humans 1

We've looked at how evolution has shaped our brains over eons. And we've taken a trip down memory lane to understand how technology has shaped each modern generation. You know this already: We are living in the most technologically advanced era in the entire history of humanity. We've got AI writing poetry, complex surgeries performed by robots, and a device in our pocket that connects us to literally everyone and everything.

We have more information now than at any other point in human existence. So, here's the million-dollar question, the one that keeps therapists busy and anti-anxiety Pharma in business:

| Why then are we so anxious and depressed?

The Evolution Gap: When Technology Outpaces Humanity

What if technology grew at a wild, untamed pace, but we humans didn't? What if we created gadgets and a lifestyle to "assist" us that now utterly outweighs our actual human capacity? What if, instead of making us healthier, it starts to consume what makes us human?

You see, we've got these two titanic forces at play: human evolution and technological evolution. And guess what? They're operating on vastly different timelines. It's like comparing a tortoise to a cheetah. While human evolution is glacial, technology is advancing faster than you can say "software update."

We're wired for connection. In a tribal sense, that used to mean our immediate community. But now, social media creates this illusion of hyper-connection, where we're constantly seeking validation from external sources—from likes and comments. This can disconnect us from our internal reality, from that still, small voice within.

And what does that do? It can fragment our identity. We start to define ourselves by external metrics, by the avatars we project online. We become addicted to the dopamine rush of notifications, constantly seeking that next hit, that next moment of external gratification.

Think about smartphones. These devices are like extensions of our hands, our minds. We're constantly plugged in, bombarded with information, with stimuli. This can keep us in a state of chronic stress, in a state of fight or flight. Our energy becomes scattered, fragmented. We lose our ability to focus, to go deep, to access that meditative state where true creativity and insight arise.

Has the Servant Become the Master?

What if technology was here to serve humans, but instead, we became its servant?

We are addicted to its conveniences–turn-by-turn navigation, personalized shopping algorithms, and the constant hit of external validation via the tiny screen in our pockets–yet we rarely measure the side effects. Is this technology leading us to a greater connection with our true selves and our infinite potential, or are we becoming increasingly disconnected, fragmented, and enslaved to the external world? We risk becoming victims of our own creations, fostering a world defined by isolation, anxiety, and dependence.

This vulnerability to distraction isn't new. Dr. Norman Doidge, in The Brain that Changes Itself, observed this shift as early as the 1960s. When the television first debuted as a window to the world, teachers began reporting that their students—even the top performers—were exhibiting signs of Attention Deficit Disorder. This happened decades ago, before color TV, the internet, or smartphones. If a simple black-and-white screen had that effect, what is the impact of today's constant digital demands?

Be Your Own Adjudicator – John Wick Style

Picture this: You're watching a John Wick movie. I mean, insane gunfire, obscene weaponry, absurd stunts – it's all visceral. You feel the reverb of those shots in your ears, in your head, in your whole body. You cringe when he gets hit. And yeah, you even get that tug at your heart when Dog climbs into the taxi.

Now, do you think your brain is just sitting there, passively observing? No way! Your brain doesn't really know the difference between that movie and reality. Why? Because your emotions are involved. Your breathing changes, your heart rate elevates. You feel that anger, that sense of justification, that adrenaline. And your mind? It interprets that as real.

Think about it. Everything we expose ourselves to elicits a response. It's not just movies; it's the news on TV, those posts on social media, those reels, those Netflix series. And if you're like most people, what are you watching? It's exciting, scary, violent, or even pornographic. It's adrenaline-inducing, anger-rousing stuff, not some soothing trickle of pristine water over mossy rocks. Am I right?

And you know what? Your brain thinks IT's ALL REAL. So, it adapts. It rewires itself to handle that anger, that stress, that constant stimulation. That's **Neuroplasticity**, man. That's the brain's remarkable ability to create new pathways to adapt to whatever stimuli you throw at it.

The key is to become conscious, to become mindful of how we're using these technologies. To use them as tools, not as crutches. To remember that our true power emanates from within, in our ability to connect to that field of infinite potential, to create our reality – our movie – from the inside out.

Escaping the Default of Negativity

What if we could transcend the Default of Negativity? What if we don't have to blindly follow the ancient dictates of evolution, technology, or even society? This survival script, after all, might be severely outdated, and it could take decades, even centuries, for this default setting to shift towards one of calm positivity.

What if it won't change until you make the choice to do so yourself?

Big Breath: Reprogramming the Default

This is the secret Runners have known for millennia. It's not just about the miles, the speed work, the VO2 max. Those are all crucial, but it's what's between the ears that elevates runners. I'm talking about mental mastery.

This is what runners do. They ignore the default program and pave a new one of their own. They refuse to stick to the negative program. The negative script. They ignore the Stress program and code a new one. They intentionally refuse the old anxiety paradigm and create a new code. One that enables them to focus their intensity on breath, rhythm and meeting their goal – to finish, to win, to be a hero.

Here's How:

Positive Self-Talk & Mantras: This is HUGE. That little voice in your head? Make it your best ally. Runners replace doubt with steel-sharp affirmations. "I am strong. I am fast. I can handle this challenge." Because the body believes what the mind tells it.

Insider Story:

When I ran my first half marathon, it was September in Kauai. Two words: hot and steamy! I was going through the first glimmers of perimenopause and let me tell you I was overheating! With the Kauai humidity (The wettest place on earth!) I knew I had to regulate my body temperature. So I used a technique I've often utilized in Reiki. I told my body you are relaxed. You are cool. We have enough air in our lungs. Enough blood to keep all the muscles smooth and relaxed. I finished the race! I didn't break any records but I completed my first half marathon. And I didn't burn out or collapse from heat fatigue. I told my body we're fine, we're cool, we have all the oxygen we need. And it believed me and rewarded me with an exquisite adventure.

Shifting Focus: When discomfort sets in, they might shift their attention to their surroundings – the trees, the sky, the rhythm of their feet on the pavement, or even distract themselves by counting or playing mental games. This breaks the cycle of negative internal rumination.

Anticipating and Naming the Negative Voice: Experienced runners know the negative thoughts are coming. They don't get surprised by them. Some even give their inner critic a name ("Oh, there's Tiffany again, worrying that my meniscus is on the verge of tearing!"). By externalizing it, they create a separation, making it easier to acknowledge the thought without becoming the thought.

Breaking it Down (Chunking): Instead of thinking about the entire 26 mile run, they break it into smaller, manageable chunks. "Just get to that next lamppost." "Just finish this mile." "Just run for five more minutes." This makes the task feel less overwhelming to the brain.

Insider Story:

When we were running Leadville Marathon my husband told me we had only 3 miles to go. It was actually 5 miles to the finish line, but to my oxygen-depleted brain, less was a cinch.

Goal Setting (Process vs. Outcome): While the finish line is the big goal, runners focus on process goals – nailing their hydration, maintaining a consistent pace, or sticking to their training schedule. These small, controllable victories build confidence and reinforce the positive habit loop.

We will get deeply entrenched with all of these techniques in the upcoming chapters. Till then, understand this–runners don't just run; they actively train their brains. They don't wait for evolution to catch up; they proactively rewire their own neural pathways, choosing to focus their intensity on their goal, their breath, their rhythm, and their power to be a hero, one intentional step at a time. It's an incredible demonstration of applied neuroplasticity!

You can only engage your mind for optimal performance, when you have mastered the mindset. When you master your mental fitness, you not only reduce negativity, you open the door to immeasurable benefits. It's science, it's discipline, and it's the key to unlocking your full potential.

And these techniques work for athletes, teachers, students, professionals regardless of age. Because whether you're an intern reading this in a coffee shop, or jetting to China and listening on wireless earbuds the message is the same: Your mind is here to serve you. Give it something amazing to create.

- Here's your Finisher medal for learning how we are wired for negativity in order to survive.

- You learned you can change your script the moment you wake up.

- You figured out why your brain is obsessed with safety

- You examined how Technology makes us negative.

- You found people who have escaped from the Default setting, and how you can too.

- You discovered Your Mindset Archetype.

- You grasped how Technology is outpacing Humanity.

- You uncovered ways to Reprogram the Default.

Are you hungry for more miles? Do you crave more ideas to be mentally fit?

Are you ready to stop surviving your life and create the movie, the reality of your dreams?

See you at the next chapter.

CHAPTER 3

COURAGE TO BREAK FROM THE TRIBE

We all get sold the story. You know the one: life unfolds in a predictable sequence, a well-worn path laid out by invisible societal and authoritarian norms. You grow up, go to school, get a degree or learn a trade that sets you on the course to become a solopreneur or land a "dream" job with epic investor payouts. Maybe you spend a small fortune on a wedding, pop out some adorable tiny humans, then settle down in a cozy condo, a McMansion, or even a life-on-the-road RV. You cruise into old age, retire, hopefully cash in on your Social Security before it vanishes into thin air, and then... you kick the bucket.

This narrative feels so ingrained, so... real.

But here's the kicker: What if that "real life story" is just a giant illusion? A perception meticulously curated and spoon-fed to us, generation after generation, by literally anyone with an ounce authority —from your well-meaning parents to news anchors, devout Church communities, celebrity idols, government officials, and even the "experts" hawking their advice on podcasts?

What if these perfectly well-meaning folks were just blindly following a script they were handed, totally oblivious that other, wildly different ways to live, create, and shine even existed? What if they didn't know that a more authentic, fulfilling existence lies just beyond those "accepted" boundaries? And what if it is known only to those rebellious, magnificent souls who dare to venture off the well-trodden track?

The Plot Twist: Tribal Instinct

Just as we are wired towards negativity, there's an ancient, primal instinct to stick with the tribe. To find safety in numbers, to cling to shared beliefs like they're life rafts in a stormy sea. Well, back in the day, when dodging sabretooth tigers was a daily agenda item, that impulse to blend in, to find safety in numbers and shared beliefs, served our ancestors well. Survival literally hinged on group cohesion.

But here's the mind-bending twist: In our gloriously complex, wildly modern world, that very same instinct can paradoxically become the chains that bind us! It can keep you from unlocking your unique, magnificent potential and experiencing a life lived absolutely on your own terms. Talk about a cosmic prank, right?

Now, don't get bent. Breaking away from a tribal mindset isn't about severing ties with your community or tossing your core values out the window. You absolutely don't have to diss your family reunions (although if you need an excuse…). You don't have to stop playing hoops with your college buddies, nix Hallmark night with your bestie, or boycott the AARP golf trip. This isn't about isolation; it's about liberation.

Here's the Magic Trick

The magic happens when you bravely step beyond those self-imposed tribal lines. Suddenly, your entire perception switches from black-and-white to glorious Technicolor. Doors swing open that were previously invisible because your ingrained programming insisted they weren't for you. Opportunities you never would have dared to contemplate appear on your radar, simply because you're no longer limited by what "your people" approve of. This shift allows you to recognize kindred spirits in unexpected places, forging powerful connections that spark new ideas, new ventures, and a richer, more vibrant life.

The cold, hard truth is that we're simply not taught to question these limits in the first place. Even worse:

| We're taught the script, not how to rewrite it.

The Tribe's Core Mission? It's You

Okay let's get into this "tribe" thing. Because even the flashiest, most champagne-soaked tribes need a job. A purpose.

And talk about pressure! Remember the old-school peer pressure? I can't even begin to imagine what it's like now. We're talking media – social and news. Misinformation. Disinformation. Full-frontal lies. Straight-up bullying. And let's not forget the "bad actors" getting paid to study your every move, just so they can hit you where it hurts most: right in the soul. And these "bad actors" aren't just cyber thieves in some far-off country, either. Nope. They're your daughter's former friends. Your son's field hockey teammates. This crap is personal.

Now, I live in Bergen County, NJ. Yeah, that Bergen County. The original Housewives stomping ground. I'm talking about living near those very towns where they sashay around, hitting up the same restaurants, shopping in the same glam stores. I was even in La Jolla at a conference last year, and when the shopkeeper heard I was from Jersey, she practically shrieked! "Oh my God," she said, "they were just in here shopping two days ago!" Like she'd spotted an extinct woolly mammoth or something.

The Housewives phenomenon tells me a lot about the tribe. We all have this burning need to be Seen. To be Heard. *We Long to Belong*. Craving to be acknowledged for what makes us unique. It's all about getting that validation, that nod from the tribe, that confirms: "Yup, you exist. You're here. You're not just part of the show. You ARE the show."

The Cozy Cage of "Survival Mode"

Sure, you're accepted. You've got your little spot on the couch, you know exactly where the snacks are, and everyone kinda gets you. It's cozy, it's safe. But here's the gut-punch truth: "safe" is just another word for "stuck." When you cling to the tribe's rules, their fears, their collective comfort zone, you're not actually living. You're just... surviving.

Think of it like this: your negative mind, bless its well-intentioned but misguided heart, is constantly trying to keep you "safe" by holding you back from anything that feels remotely risky. Well, guess what? Your tribe often does the exact same thing. Their unspoken job? To make sure you simply survive. To keep you from rocking the boat, from making waves, from doing anything that might make them uncomfortable.

But here's the real question, you magnificent trailblazer: Is "mere survival" enough for you? If you're genuinely happy just cruising along, blending in, and hitting the bare minimum, then kudos! More power to Ya. But if that little voice inside you is screaming for more—for a quest, for growth, for a life that feels less like a high school play and more like your own masterpiece—then you need an exit strategy.

You've got to find that other zone, the one where true, exhilarating, messy, joyful LIVING happens. Because you, my friend, are not just here to survive. You're here to transform. So, is "just getting by" truly enough for a seeker like you?

Remember, we're taught the script, not how to rewrite it. So, is survival truly enough for a Transformer like you?

The Drama Defense: A Distraction from Destiny

Oh, the little dramas we allow to hijack our lives! Your dad's auto insurance lapsed and his policy won't renew (true story, I know!). Or you've got that niggling twitch in your left breast you've been meaning to get checked out for months. Maybe you've been handed the soul-crushing task of laying off 25% of your team, and it's eating you alive, turning your stomach into a knot of dread.

These scenarios? They're annoying. They're stressful. And they suck up a LOT of your precious time and mental energy. But here's the real gut punch: In allowing these dramas to consume our lives, we're actually throwing up a giant roadblock to our real purpose. It sounds like this:

- I can't possibly apply for that manager role. (Because I only meet 8 out of 10 requirements, and perfection is the enemy of progress.)

- Oh, I can't possibly take those piano lessons now. (even though you secretly crave the applause of a piano recital).

- I can't start learning agentic AI workflows. (Because I'm too old to pick up a new skill, and the Tribe loves to tell me my peak passed years ago.)

- I can't write that book; there are already too many flooding the market. (Ahem!)

- What if I fail the Sommelier test? What if I can't tell the difference between a Chianti and a Cab? (Spoiler: No one cares, and the world keeps spinning.)

- I can't meditate. I'm too busy worrying about AFib. (So, you're choosing chaos over two minutes of peace. Smart.)

We fill our lives with drama precisely because it's a convenient distraction from following our true purpose. It's easier that way, don't you know? This way, I won't get crushed by those common fears of inadequacy, ageism, and conflict avoidance. I won't make an ass of myself. I won't…

How about this? You won't live your true destiny.

> *"Most Men Will Die with Their Dreams Still Inside Them"*
> *– Anthony Astbury*

By focusing all your energy on external noise, you successfully avoid facing the terrifying, magnificent internal work required to build the life you truly want.

This is what coach and founder of the Whole Man Academy, Anthony Astbury, warns us. The real consequence of allowing the drama, and the fear, to serve as your master keeps you safe, small, and guaranteed to expire with your greatest potential untouched.

The Tribe's Accidental Gift

Sometimes, the tribe shows you exactly what you DON'T WANT. And that, sweet pea, is just as crucial as knowing what you do want.

Take my dad, bless his practical, salt-of-the-earth heart. This guy was the eldest of seven and took his familial duty seriously. The burden of responsibility and expectation, inherited from his father—who was himself an outlier – kind of replaced romance with practicality in his sweet, sensible DNA.

Hence, every single wedding anniversary, his ritual was set in stone: Dad would stop at the grocery store, grab one of those over-the-top, flowery Victorian cards, scribble his signature, and enclose a check—a whopping twenty-dollar check—to his wife. A check! For the woman who birthed his children and kept the world spinning.

And I knew right then and there: I never, ever wanted to feel practical in a relationship. I wanted to feel cherished, even if it was just one day out of the year.

Fast forward to my parent's 50th anniversary. My brother and I were planning a huge celebration—I even drove a massive, three-tier wedding cake from a famous bakery in New Jersey. But the atmosphere was shadowed by Mom's quiet melancholy over never owning an engagement ring. In our culture, the solemnity of the marriage and the joining of two families was a greater bond than a single piece of jewelry.

As the anniversary loomed, I cornered Dad during a routine trip to Costco. "Look, Dad!" I feigned shock, pointing dramatically at the jewelry counter. "An eternity band! It's on sale!" (because honestly, isn't everything at Costco on sale?).

My usually soft-spoken dad was cornered. He knew I wasn't budging until that ring was purchased. After some internal, economical calculations, he offered, "It looks like a good bargain, no?"

"It is," I breathed, letting out a genuine sigh of relief. The ring was purchased and a little piece of the fairytale was finally secured.

A Golden Triumph, A Lasting Memory

The air practically buzzed with celebration. This wasn't just any party; it was a family triumph, a joyous gathering for my parents' 50th anniversary. Friends and family poured in, all eager to shower the couple with love and good wishes for five decades of matrimonial victory.

My brother, ever the sentimental softie, showed up with 50 perfect red roses. Dad, in his wonderfully solemn way, presented them to Mom, an apology and a testament to 50 years together. The aunts, bless their hearts, had orchestrated an Indian feast, served buffet style, filling the air with intoxicating aromas and vibrant colors.

The wedding cake was, of course, the star of the show, eliciting oohs and aahs from everyone. Mom and Dad, looking every bit like giddy newlyweds, coyly cut the cake, giggling as if it were their very first slice together. And Mom, her face beaming, proudly wore her ring. Earlier that day, Dad had given her a card, and with a sly, bemused twinkle in her eye, Mom had playfully asked, "No check?"

That, my friends, was their last anniversary together. The very next year, Mom died suddenly and tragically.

And what's etched in my memory above all else? It's not the twenty-dollar check she joked about. Not at all. What I remember most is the breaking of old patterns, the forging of new ones that finally fulfilled wishes. It was never about the check. Never the check.

Really Good Question to Ask # 2

We've seen how the tribe gives you a job. How it keeps you from doing the things you would love to do. That brings me to the second big question to ask.

| Who Is Your Master?

The Secret Sauce Question

When I worked in luxury automotive, we constantly faced demands from the corporate home office to launch global campaigns that felt detached from what our local, discerning customers actually wanted. The pressure to conform to that external authority—the brand directives—was immense, but the risk of alienating the client base was even greater.

To cut through that noise and determine the true customer journey, I developed a simple secret sauce: It isn't what Marketing *thinks*. It's what the Customer *needs*. I learned the hard way when the servant takes direction from the wrong master, the outcome can be disastrous.

This corporate question leads to a far more important personal one: Who is your master? Seriously. Are you taking direction from an external force—

someone you've given your ultimate authority to—like your boss, your spouse, your parents, or even a set of outdated self-imposed limitations?

The Consensus Trap: Why Outliers Win

Listen, we're hardwired for the Tribe. We crave consensus, agreement, and the safety of the herd. Our brains treat social exclusion like physical pain—it's the ultimate survival mechanism. But if you want a life that's 10x better than the default, you have to find the courage to break the consensus. The most extraordinary returns on life happen outside the warm, safe bubble of agreement.

Here are a few people who chose to be their own master and broke from the Tribe.

Martin Luther: The Power of the Page

In the 16th century, the ultimate power structure was the Catholic Church. They sold salvation as Indulgences and demanded total obedience. Martin Luther, a lone frustrated monk looked at this and said "hard pass." His weapon wasn't an army, but a single sheet of paper: The 95 Theses, which he audaciously hammered onto a church door of a German church to defy the entire religious establishment. His contribution? Emphasis on individual faith, independent of intermediaries, and the supreme importance of scripture, ignited the Protestant Reformation. This seismic event irrevocably altered the course of European history, religion, and politics, shaping the religious landscape of the Western world as we know it. One man, one radical idea, and 95 theses changed everything.

Coco Chanel: Breaking the Fabric Ceiling

In the rigid high-fashion world of the 1920s, the ruling Tribe was clear: a woman's place was to be physically restricted, corseted, and draped in uncomfortable, impractical silks. Gabrielle "Coco" Chanel didn't just *stomp* out of that convention—she threw a grenade at it. She was mocked as a rebel for championing simple, fluid, and comfortable designs inspired by menswear, like the tweed jacket and jersey fabric. Her contemporaries saw this as heresy. But Chanel saw female freedom and self-mastery. She understood that restricting a woman's body restricts her mind. By liberating women from the corset, she gave them the physical and mental ability to move, work, and compete in the modern world. Today, her brand is not just linked to *haute couture* (high fashion) but is synonymous with timeless, non-conformist elegance, a global empire built entirely on ignoring the old rules of the fashion Tribe.

Galileo Galilei: The Universe's Truth-Teller

The geocentric view of the universe was gospel in 1610. And here comes Galileo, daring to champion the heliocentric model – the sun is the center, not earth, you narcissistic humans! His unwavering support for this revolutionary idea wasn't just a scientific disagreement; it directly challenged the deeply entrenched religious and scientific authority of his era. His insistence on cold, hard empirical evidence and scientific reasoning didn't just revolutionize our understanding of astronomy; it literally paved the way for the scientific method that underpins all modern scientific inquiry. Because of Galileo, we know we're no longer the center of the universe. Humbling, right?

My Great Escape: How I Ditched the Tribe's "Normal"

I've never been an endurance girl. The idea of running a marathon was so far off my radar it wasn't even a flicker on my bucket list. I was perfectly content with my routine: tennis, HIIT, and kickboxing. That was my safe, comfortable fitness Tribe.

Then I met Wayne. And the dude rolls in with a proposition: "Look," he says, with that intense runner's gaze, "we can travel to the coolest places on Earth, the most adventurous corners, but you're going to have to run with me."

Now running with him meant keeping pace with a guy who casually logged daily mileage and fit in a marathon once a month. Yeah, my new reality. Wayne, the seasoned "Marathon Whisperer," quickly assessed my fitness. After upgrading my shoes, he delivered the verdict: "You're in pretty good shape. There's no reason you can't run a marathon. A piece of cake."

A piece of cake, my ass!

My Unlikely Ascent: From Spectator to Finisher

We trained four to five times a week, steadily increasing our distances from five to seven miles, and beyond. The physical conditioning—strengthening my endurance, increasing my lung capacity—was one thing, but the magic was the relationship we forged. Out in nature, trotting past rivers, streets, and parks, we spent hours just talking, laughing, and truly getting to know each other. Bonding while clocking miles was absolutely incredible. I didn't know it then, but I was already tapping into that Marathon Mindset, becoming clearer, more fluid, and blissfully less stressed.

Our training runs became mini-adventures, exploring urban jungles and serene escapes alike:

- Central Park, NYC: 6 miles of the gorgeous but deceptively hilly loop. And a treat to run the shorter reservoir loop where countless movies have been filmed.

- Bear Mountain Loop Trail: 3.7 miles of climbing up trails and rock slabs on a teeny portion of the Appalachian Trail.

- Cape May Boardwalk: Four miles, out and back of soothing, pancake-flat relief.

Then there's my favorite–Sleepy Hollow, Rockefeller Preserve State Park. 45 miles of scenic carriage roads, shared by runners and horses. We'd start with the gentle two-mile Aqueduct Trail warm-up, before hitting the heart of the run: the 13 Bridges Trail. It was 2.8 miles of pure canopy magic, jogging past thirteen charming, old-fashioned bridges. So charming, you almost forgot you were sweating like a wild boar.

Quick break at the visitor center for water refills, bathroom breaks, and maybe a peek at the latest Artist exhibiting at the gallery. Because even marathon training deserves a cultural interlude.

From there, the trail demanded grit: the long loop included an agonizing, beautiful climb up Buttermilk Hill, followed by an exhilarating downhill stretch with reservoir views. Past the scenic Union Church of Pocantico Hills (you must stop and ask to see the Chagall stained-glass window!). We'd finish our 12.8-mile adventure with a final uphill grind—roughly 2 hours of running, hiking, and existential questioning.

I loved it. I was getting stronger, hammering descents with confidence and acclimating to the weather. Now, east coast humidity? That's not just sweat, people; it's a training technique that tricks your body into thinking it's running at elevation. I learned humidity parallels elevation, which gave me a leg up in oxygen-depleted altitude.

By this time Wayne was ready to drop his real bombshell: Honolulu Marathon. My mind had gotten used to the long, hot reality of a marathon, but the destination—Honolulu—was the ultimate lure!

The Tribe's Chorus of Negativity

My tribe however, wasn't as enthusiastic. My nearest and dearest were like "Huh?" And then, because we're all so good at projecting our own fear they dropped these classics:

- You're going to destroy your knees! All that pounding on the pavement means you'll need a hip replacement by Christmas!

- You better be careful. You could get heat stroke out in the sun for so long. Your mother's side is prone to strokes.

- You're going to hit the wall and just collapse! You know, where your body just shuts down and you can't move? What if no one finds you?!

And my personal favorite:

- What do you have to prove?

The tribe means well. They love you, and they're just projecting their own anxieties about pushing boundaries onto your magnificent endeavor. But that's exactly why you're doing it. To prove them (and maybe a tiny part of your own self) wrong.

Finish Line, A Transformed Me

We landed in Honolulu and checked into the Sheraton, perfectly positioned for the 5:00 AM start. The convention center was a buzzing hive for bib and swag collection, and we performed the sacred pre-race ritual of carb loading on a mountain of noodles.

The air at the start line was electric. At five sharp, a burst of gleeful pyrotechnics exploded overhead, launching us into the race like a celebration. Honolulu's course is unique: a glorious, festive parade of professional athletes mixed with costume-clad enthusiasts. We saw Christmas elves, couples in wedding attire, and a Samurai clattering the course in wooden sandals.

We cruised downtown in the inky dark, fueled by generous bystanders handing out tea. But as the sun cast its golden glow over Diamond Head Lighthouse, and we hit the infamous out-and-back stretch of Kalanianaole Highway, I hit The Wall hard.

It wasn't just physical exhaustion; it was the mind-numbing tedium. My legs still moved, but my mind staged a full-scale revolt. My inner voice screamed: "You have nothing left. You've been doing this for hours. Look how far you have to go—it's the exact same stretch you just ran, only hotter. Just stop." My energy dropped, my focus evaporated, and the beautiful scenery dissolved into a monotonous, endless strip of asphalt.

Wayne recognized the sudden shift from physical effort to psychological crisis. He deployed his famous antidote: "You're fine. It's just a few more miles to the finish." He knew the profound truth forged over thousands of miles: The Wall is all in your head. It's not a physical depletion of glycogen; it's the brain quitting long before the body does. Just like every other self-imposed barrier we create.

We slogged through the sun, grateful for every water break and every random cheer. The final leg included the soul-crushing incline up to Diamond Head, quickly followed by a breathtaking downhill stretch with sweeping, wave-riding ocean views. This view fueled the final push through lush Kapiolani Park.

Then, there it was: the Finish Line! We burst through the balloon banner, our names called out triumphantly. A volunteer placed the finisher medal around my neck, and I wore it like a solid gold Oscar.

I ran a marathon. And I had just turned 50.

Runners are Wired to Split from the Tribe

So, what's the deal with runners, you ask? Why do these crazy people keep lacing up their Hokas and hitting the pavement like it's their job? Well, it's not some grand philosophical quest they try to embark on. It just… happens.

They slap on those shoes, they hit the road or trail, and they start running. They're breathing, man. They're watching their steps, dodging rogue tree roots, avoiding cracks in the pavement, sidestepping other humans, maybe even giving a dirty look to the occasional car that veers too close.

And in that moment? They can't focus on anything else. There's no room for that snarky comment your "friend" made at the last dinner party. No space for the existential dread of your kid flunking the math final. All their energy is consumed in staying right there, in the oxygen-rich moment. Their breathing settles into a repetitive, easy rhythm. Their steps feel almost effortless. Best of all? That giant wall of chaos that usually clutters their minds? Poof. Gone.

And just like that, their heart and mind are in glorious harmony.

The Zen of the Jog: Hacking Your Own Operating System

What these running rebels are doing, often without even realizing it, is creating what the fancy science folks call harmonious alignment. It's when their heart rhythms, brain waves, nervous system, and breathing all lock into a synchronized state of physiological functioning. It's like their entire being is finally singing the same awesome tune.

Think about it: when you're stressed, anxious, or just plain pissed off, your heart rhythm is doing a jagged, garbled dance. It's sending all kinds of panicked signals to your brain, making it impossible to think straight, focus, or do anything but react in full-blown "fight or flight" mode. You know that one, right? The one that keeps you stuck.

But when you're running, when your mind is too busy to even see that wall of chaos, it shifts into a more natural, powerful rhythm. Studies shout it from the rooftops: your emotions profoundly impact your heart rhythms, and those heart rhythms, in turn, send powerful signals right back to your brain, shaping your thoughts, your feelings, and even how well you perform at life.

Runners, through the sheer, repetitive act of putting one foot in front of the other, are combining all the vital factors that reduce stress and negativity. They're tapping into the intrinsic connection between physical movement and a profound sense of mental clarity, even liberation. Remember that old program that keeps whispering negative nonsense? These guys have found the key to erase that old programming, and with it, unlock the freedom of a peaceful mind.

So no, this isn't just about pounding pavement. It's about hacking your own operating system, one glorious, synchronized step at a time.

| Runners Meditate in Motion

Other Champs Who Nail the Internal Harmony

So, who else is in on this secret sauce of heart-mind alliance? Turns out, plenty of indomitable humans have figured out how to get their systems humming in harmony:

Mind/Body Sync Masters: From Zen monks and Vipassana devotees to Yoga and Martial Arts masters, the goal is the same: find stillness in the action. They deliberately train their nervous system to chill the heck out, using breath and controlled movement to achieve an almost unbelievable level of internal command.

Flow State Channelers: This is the high-stakes crew—surgeons, fighter pilots, musicians lost in a symphony, and ER doctors. Under extreme duress, they achieve a superhuman level of focus where action, emotion, and precision perfectly align. They aren't trying; they are channeling pure, effortless flow.

Vibe Cultivators: These are the positive emotion powerhouses. Folks who practice daily gratitude, feel deep connection, and immerse themselves in genuine joy. These potent emotions instantly pull your entire physical and mental system into sync. They aren't begging the Universe for a break; they are broadcasting abundance.

The common thread? An uncanny ability to regulate their inner chaos. They are consciously cultivating a beautiful, harmonious rhythm that defeats the default noise.

Consider this famously pragmatic saying which appeared on Nike t-shirts in the 1980s, motivated by the no-nonsense ethos of Nike founder Bill Bowerman. Take that for a decidedly legitimate reason to hit the pavement.

| Running is Cheaper than Therapy

Trailblazers: Runners Who Shattered the Status Quo

When it comes to runners who didn't just run, but utterly shattered the expectations of their "tribe," a few names immediately leap to mind. These are the individuals who redefined what was possible, not just with their legs, but with their sheer force of will.

Steve Prefontaine: 'Pre' was the embodiment of breaking from the pack. His aggressive, all-out racing style was a stark departure from the more conservative tactics prevalent in his era. He didn't run to conform; he ran to impose his will, inspiring a generation with his unwavering "give it all you've got" attitude.

Grete Waltz: Her story is the definition of an accidental conqueror. She was a superb Norwegian track athlete who initially disliked the marathon format, preferring the 800m and 1500m. She had no love for the grueling endurance challenge—in fact, she reportedly hated the marathon. She ran the 1978 New York City Marathon reluctantly, but despite feeling unprepared, she not only won but shattered the world record by over two minutes. This accidental conquest immediately transformed her from a mid-distance runner into the first global female marathon superstar, fundamentally changing the world's perception of women's endurance capabilities.

François D'Haene: A titan of the ultra-trail world, François D'Haene has dominated the most prestigious mountain races, including an incredible four victories at the Ultra-Trail du Mont-Blanc (UTMB). His thoughtful, balanced approach to life – as a winemaker and father – combined with his relentless pursuit of extreme mountain challenges, exemplifies a deep connection between physical endeavor and personal fulfillment.

Your Freedom Blueprint

And that, my friend, is exactly the energy we're channeling here. You've seen what these incredible runners achieve when they shed the "tribe's" limiting beliefs. Now, are you ready to harness that power for your own life? Let's figure out how to hit the mute button on that ancient drama. This isn't some mystical hocus pocus; it's a deliberate, step-by-step process of reprogramming your brain's default settings.

The Outlier Operating System: 4 Steps to Break the Tribe

The "rebel runner" mindset isn't just for athletes; it's a universal skill. Apply these pillars whether you're logging miles or just logging into your laptop.

1. Courage to Be an Outlier – The Breakaway

This is the gutsy decision to break from the pack and forge your own track. Conformity is the true sin that holds you back from your magnificent potential. It's choosing your difficult path, even when the Tribe labels it "crazy" or irrelevant. Whether you're the executive defending a radical new vision in the boardroom or the runner opting for monster hill repeats in the pouring rain, your goal is defiance. The comfort of the pack is the enemy of excellence. Your unique vision is worth the discomfort of being the only one heading in that direction.

2. Radical Self-Awareness – The Internal GPS

Become a detective of your own mind by activating your Personal BS Detector. Like the ultrarunner who feels the searing burn in their quads and pivots from the immediate thought "I can't!" to the strategic question "What is this pain telling me?" you learn to tune in. Catch yourself when you're mindlessly scrolling to avoid something or saying, "I'm not qualified." Pause, and ask: "Is this thought an actual limit, or just my old, tired default programming?" You gain the power to distinguish the genuine fence from the perceived illusion.

3. Fierce Questioning of Beliefs – Unlearning

This is gaining the power to challenge every inherited assumption you carry. Look at those invisible rules handed down by the Tribe and ask: "Says who?" Just as the runner refuses to accept the fatalistic belief of "I always hit the wall at Mile 20," you must challenge ingrained narratives like "I'm not good with money" or "I always fail at launching." Become your own chief investigator and replace the limiting story with the powerful, defiant question: **Why not me?** Refuse to carry beliefs simply because they feel familiar.

4. Unshakeable Authenticity – The Sovereign Edge

This is the ultimate prize: living in unapologetic alignment with your inner truth. Your daily actions must match your core values. Like the authentic runner who dictates their own pace and listens only to their body's spirit, you protect your peace. You set boundaries that serve your purpose, even if it disappoints someone else. This is where you celebrate your inner Nutty Professor and unleash your Sovereign Identity. This inner fulfillment is the only score that truly matters.

The Bannister Effect: Shattering the Impossible

Fascinating is how we swallow the story, assume the tribe has set the bar correctly. But then you have the outliers who do their thing, and presto chango! The assumption, the mythical pinnacle crumbles.

This, my friend, is called the Bannister Effect. It's a phenomenon where a breakthrough achievement, previously thought to be impossible, inspires others to quickly achieve or even surpass that same feat. It demonstrates that perceived limitations are often more psychological than physical. Once a barrier is broken, a massive mental shift occurs, allowing many to follow.

Now the Bannister Effect isn't just some dusty historical footnote; it's living proof that your perceived limits are often just a pile of mental garbage you've allowed yourself to believe. Once ONE bad-ass blasts through what everyone thought was impossible, it totally rewires our collective brain, unleashing a tidal wave of "holy crap, I can do that too!"

Here are some classic examples of "Bannisters" that have been well and truly Banished:

The 4-Minute Mile: From "Nope" to "Next!"

For decades, running a mile in under four minutes was considered so out-of-bounds, doctors were practically writing prescriptions for "less ambition." But then, on May 6, 1954, Roger Bannister said, "Hold my beer," and clocked it in 3 minutes, 59.4 seconds. Within weeks, his record was toast, and in just two-and-a-half years, ten more runners blew past the four-minute mark. Now? Thousands do it, including a bunch of high school kids. Bannister didn't just break a physical barrier; he shattered a mental one for the entire planet. What's your 4-minute mile?

The 30 MPH Speed Limit: Faster Than a Speeding BulletC

Back in early days of the automobile, people actually believed the human body would disintegrate if you went faster than 30 MPH. Seriously! So, speed limits were set accordingly. But then, as cars got faster and people, shockingly, didn't explode, that ridiculous psychological barrier dissolved faster than your New Year's resolutions. Now we cruise at 70 MPH without batting an eye. What ridiculous "speed limit" are you putting on your own life?

Women's Marathon: Smashing the 2:20 Ceiling

For years, the women's marathon record stubbornly clung to that 2-hour, 20-minute mark, a mental fortress for elite female runners. But then, a wave of undeterred women, led by the utterly relentless Paula Radcliffe, came along and said, "Nope." Radcliffe's aggressive, no-holds-barred pacing didn't just break the record; she obliterated it with a time of 2:15.25, inspiring a whole new generation. Today, breaking 2:20 isn't just a dream; it's a testament to what happens when you decide the "impossible" is just a suggestion.

Personal Computers: Your Own Command Center!

Remember when computers were just for eggheads in labs, controlled by arcane codes and looking like giant refrigerators? The idea of "a computer in every home" was pure science fiction. But then, Apple's Macintosh in 1984 dropped, waving its little mouse and flashing its user-friendly Graphical User Interface (GUI). It was like magic! It proved computers could be fun, intuitive, and for everyone. Suddenly, the "impossible" became the norm. You're now reading this on a device that descended from that breakthrough. What seemingly "impossible" are you about to make your new normal?

Rules of Road

- Here's your finisher medal for getting through the myth of the Tribe.

- You've seen how the tribe uses peer pressure, survival mode and safety to keep you locked into copilot mode.

- You contemplated Really Good Question #2: Who is Your Master?

- You met some Outliers who had the courage to escape the Tribe

- You learned the Runners Secret: Harmonious Alignment of the heart and mind

- You learned the 4 Step Blueprint to Break from the Tribe

- You banished the Bannister Effect

Are you ready to stop surviving your life?

Let's go to the next chapter.

CHAPTER 4

IS THE VOICE IN YOUR HEAD BEING MEAN TO YOU?

This Chapter scares me. But I'm going to suck it up and lay it all out, because if even one ounce of this helps you find some solace, gives you a moment of Zen, it'll be worth it.

We live in terrifying, high-pressure times. Global power clashes, economic volatility, the rise of AI, climate chaos—every sunrise feels like more dread. The world isn't just burning; it feels like it's actively crumbling beneath our feet, ready to erupt into a fiery volcano or slide away in a devastating earthquake at any second. We may be swiping and tapping in a digital society, but deep down, doesn't it feel a lot like the darn Dark Ages?

Is Our Modern Society Just the Middle Ages in Designer Clothes?

This might sting a little, but it's time for a dose of unfiltered truth. We strut around in our fancy designer apparel, tapping on our smart screens, thinking we're so wildly evolved. But take a peek under the hood, and you might just find we're living in a slightly more sparkly version of the Middle Ages. History doesn't repeat itself exactly, but it's got a serious cyclical glitch, and right now, the pedal is hitting a little too close to home.

Who's Got All the Gold and the Land?

Back in the day, kings, queens, and religious institutions hogged all the prime real estate and pretty much all the money, leaving everyone else to toil as a peasant. Fast forward to now: we have the 1%, the tech titans, and the billionaires. They own everything from your favorite social media platform to massive chunks of physical land and a fleet of superyachts. You're still hustling your butt off, and a big percentage of your effort is funneled straight into their overflowing coffers. New labels, same old limitations. It's the exact same script, just with a fresh coat of paint.

Who's Feeding You the Truth?

In medieval times, religion and the monarchy had a chokehold on information. They told you what to believe, what to fear, and if you questioned it? Heretic! Today, you might not get burned at the stake, but you are still being fed a carefully curated diet of "truth" by massive media conglomerates, social media giants, and influencers who know exactly how to manipulate your emotional algorithms. You think you're getting the whole story? Nope, you're in a polished echo chamber that's probably just as thick with distortion as any medieval village's rumor mill.

Corporate Feudalism Is a Thing

We don't have literal lords and serfs, but what about those mega-corporations and their CEOs who wield more power than some small nations? You might have a job, but how much true autonomy do you have? How much upward mobility? You're trading your precious time and energy for a sense of security within a giant, hierarchical system. It's like modern serfdom, only instead of tilling the soil, you're pushing papers or clicking buttons.

Nature's Still Kicking Our Butt

Remember when medieval folks got totally pummeled by things like the Little Ice Age or massive famines wiped out entire villages? They didn't know why it was happening, but they sure felt the pain. Guess what? We're still getting smacked around by Mother Nature, only now we call it climate change. An inconvenient PR makeover of Global Warming after Al Gore shared the truth. Rising seas, crazy storms, dwindling resources – it's all leading to potential chaos, displacement, and conflict, just like back then. We might have scientific names for it, but the "oh crap, the sky is falling" feeling? That's timeless.

Global Plagues – Still a Problem!

The Black Death zipped across continents thanks to trade routes, showing how interconnected and vulnerable the medieval world was. Fast forward to 2020: a new virus pops up, and thanks to our glorious international travel, it circumnavigates the globe faster than you can say "social distancing." Despite all our medical marvels, the sheer speed and global reach of a pandemic proved that we're still incredibly susceptible, echoing those medieval fears. We just had better masks this time.

So, while we might have better plumbing and flashier gadgets, the fundamental struggles – who's in control, who gets what, and how we deal with things beyond our control – are still shockingly familiar. Maybe it's time to stop just surviving in this modern Middle Ages and actually start reigning over our own lives.

Welcome to the Apocalypse – Or Just Tuesday

Imagine this: You've prepped for two weeks straight for a big Board Meeting. You've done the research, crafted high-fidelity graphs and charts that could win Canva awards. You even splurged on a new tie from Neiman Marcus, way over your price range, because this tie doesn't just whisper; it shouts to the heavens: 'Behold, this man Flourisheth!'

You dominate the meeting like a Tony Robbins pro, absolutely nailing it. You even get a few claps, maybe even a silent nod of approval from the big boss. As you head out the door, already pulling out your phone to text your Boo to chill the Prosecco, a voice inside your head pipes up:

> "You're wearing the same tie as the CTO, now he's going to think you get paid too much and are trying to one-up him."

You stop mid-step, Prosecco dreams dissolving like mist. Where on earth did that come from? It's like a tiny saboteur, a vicious little imp whispering poison directly into the well of a potentially beautiful moment. Unsettling as it is, that voice has done its job, hasn't it? It's not just nudging you back; it's shoving you towards the familiar, the status quo, the comfortable, soul-sucking predictability of what you already know – even if that "safety" is actively sabotaging your joy. And just like that, doubt doesn't merely enter; it stomps in, kicks off its shoes, and hunkers down in your comfiest chair for a long stay. It growls at your girlfriend, chugs your beer, and murmurs malicious garbage in your head that makes you want to curl up and whimper.

Where does that persistent, often unwelcome, voice inside our heads actually come from? Why is it your worst enemy, instead of your best pal?

More importantly, WHY IS IT BEING SO DANG MEAN TO YOU?

The Architects of Anxiety: Meet Your Inner Demolition Crew

Let's talk about the real villains in your life – the ones living rent-free in your magnificent head. We're not talking about your grumpy boss or that dude who cuts you off in traffic and gives you the finger. We're talking about the Architects of Anxiety, those sneaky, little inner voices constantly trying to build a fortress of fear around your potential. These aren't your friends, mate. They're saboteurs.

The sooner you figure out who and what they are, the sooner you can tell them to stop whispering bitter things into your ears.

This is complex stuff, but trust me, it's worth every brain cell you burn to figure out why negativity gets planted inside you, and best of all, how to boot it out! Ready to jump in?

We're going to dive deep into three powerful constructs that are constantly shaping your inner landscape:

- Your Inner Voice
- Your Ego
- The Human Collective

I call them the Hidden Architects of Anxiety. They're the masterminds behind the mayhem, and it's time to shine a spotlight on them.

Your Inner Voice: The Megaphone for the Mayhem

You know the whisper of the negative voice intimately. The inner voice is the first perpetrator of the Architects of Anxiety. This is the running monologue in your head. It can be a helpful guide, a creative spark or, when hijacked by anxiety, it becomes really, really mean.

Think of Fleabag on Prime video. Her entire show is built around her inner voice. She's constantly breaking the fourth wall, giving us direct, hilarious, but often deeply self-deprecating commentary on her life. Her inner voice isn't just a whisper; it's a running, often sarcastic, monologue pointing out her own flaws, her terrible decisions, and the absurdity of everything around her. It's sharp, it's witty, but underneath it all, it's constantly picking apart her choices and confirming her deepest fears about herself. It's the ultimate Inner Critic with a stand-up comedy routine.

The Inner Critic can play a chorus of roles that can make your head spin:

The Inner Critic: The Naysayer

Who it is: This is the whiny, judgmental little jerk in your head that sounds suspiciously like your meanest ex, your most disapproving relative, or that voice that told you Santa wasn't real. It's the ultimate buzzkill, the party pooper of your potential.

What it does: Its sole mission is to poison your potential. It tells you you're not good enough, smart enough, pretty enough, or capable enough. It whispers that you'll fail, that everyone's judging you, and that you should probably just stay in bed with a bag of chips. Its job is to keep you "safe" by keeping you small, silent, and stuck. It thrives on past mistakes and future hypotheticals.

The Perfectionist: Mrs. Perfect-Pants

Who it is: Oh, she's a demanding tyrant, dressed in impossibly crisp clothes, carrying a clipboard, and constantly pointing out your flaws. She doesn't just want perfection; she demands it – flawless, pristine, and without even the ghost of a wrinkle.

What it does: She's the reason you never start that amazing project, or if you do, you never finish it. Why? Because it's never "good enough." She creates paralysis by analysis, making you obsess over every tiny detail until the moment for action passes. She's a fun-sucking dictator who thrives on impossible standards and the fear of making a single mistake.

The Catastrophizer: The "What If" Monster

Who it is: This is the ultimate drama queen, the Olympic gold medalist in worst-case scenarios, the Hollywood producer of your own personal horror movie. She's dark, dramatic, and always assumes the sky is about to fall.

What it does: She takes one tiny, legitimate concern and blows it up into a global catastrophe. Lost your keys? You'll be homeless. Sent a slightly awkward email? You'll be fired and shunned by society. She imagines every terrible thing that could happen, paralyzing you with fear, keeping you in a constant state of hyper-vigilance, and convincing you that every dark cloud has a tornado in it.

The Comparison Trap: The Grass-Is-Greener Gremlin

Who it is: This is the sneaky, joy-stealing little gremlin constantly lurking over your shoulder while you scroll through social media. It's whispering about how everyone else is richer, happier, thinner, more successful, and living a much more fabulous life than you.

What it does: It makes you feel utterly inadequate and constantly chases someone else's highlight reel instead of appreciating your own damn journey. It's a master of "fake news," using curated online personas to convince you that your life just doesn't measure up. Its whole purpose is to steal your joy and make you believe you're constantly falling short.

This architect, my friend is not here to protect you. It's there to keep you small, safe, and stuck in the meticulously designed misery. The good news? You're the landlord of your brain. And it's time to evict this noisy tenant.

Your Ego: The Grand Protector Who Overdoes It

Let's get to your ego, that tricky little sucker. In a nutshell, it's the part of you that's desperately trying to keep you safe, significant, and in control.

It's your self-image, your identity, your fiercely guarded place in the world. Think of it as your inner storyteller, constantly spinning tales from your experiences, memories, and wildest dreams into some kind of coherent sense of "you." Its whole job is to ensure your survival, both physically and socially. It just wants you to be accepted, avoid pain, and feel like you belong, that you matter. You spend a lifetime painstakingly crafting this identity, and trust me, there's a ton invested in it. But as we learned earlier, we often build this identity by marching down the clan's path, living the life we're "supposed" to live, not necessarily the one we were born to rock.

Now, here's where the ego can become a real pain in your perfectly sculpted ass. When it feels even remotely threatened, it can transform into a total drama queen, turning your beautiful mind into fertile ground for anxiety to bloom like a toxic weed.

- It craves approval like a hungry vampire, which leaves you a sitting duck for the Comparison Trap and that soul-sucking fear of not being enough for others.

- It absolutely hates failure with a fiery passion, pushing your Perfectionist into brutal overdrive to avoid even the slightest, most microscopic misstep.

- It needs to be in control of absolutely everything, which is why your Catastrophizer goes completely wild, trying to predict and micromanage every single hypothetical disaster that could possibly, maybe, remotely happen.

The Ego on Display: Celebrity Shenanigans

Frank Gallagher from Shameless: Frank is a masterclass in an ego that thrives on self-deception and avoiding responsibility. His "I" is built on being the smartest, the survivor, the one who can always talk his way out of trouble, even when he's clearly the cause of it. His ego fiercely protects his identity as a "free spirit" or a "victim of the system," allowing him to justify his destructive behavior and avoid facing the consequences. He's a perfect example of an ego that's so committed to its own narrative of self-preservation that it causes chaos for everyone around him.

The profound irony of course is that this very "protective" voice — this overprotective, hypercritical inner commentator — often ends up undermining your confidence, stifling your growth, and preventing you from experiencing the very connection and fulfillment the ego so desperately craves. It keeps us small, plays it safe, and it reinforces the very feelings of inadequacy it's trying to shield us from. They're like two sides of the same somewhat tarnished coin, aren't they? Understanding this deep and intricate connection can be incredibly liberating.

" We all have self-doubt. You don't deny it, but you also don't capitulate to it. You embrace it."

– Kobe Bryant

The Human Collective: The Tribe's Heavy Hand

Think for a moment about that constant hum beneath the surface of our individual thoughts. Beyond the "I," beyond that personal narrative we've been discussing, don't you feel there's something else? A kind of echo chamber of humanity residing within each one of us – a human collective voice.

Where does this come from? Well, consider our very nature as social creatures. For millennia, our survival and flourishing have depended on connection, on belonging to a group. We've evolved to be exquisitely attuned to the thoughts, feelings, and behaviors of those around us. We learn through imitation, we absorb cultural norms like air, and we are deeply influenced by the stories and beliefs passed down through generations.

This is the big one, the collective unconscious, the clan. It's all the unspoken rules, societal expectations, cultural norms, and shared fears that we soak up like SpongeBob.

In every scenario, the Human Collective at the tailgate demands conformity to unspoken group norms. It's the anxiety of not fitting in, of being seen as different or less than in the eyes of the tribe. It subtly, powerfully, tells you how you should behave to earn acceptance.

Architects of Anxiety are intricately connected. One is the messenger, one is the protector-gone-rogue, and one is the societal influence. They're like a dysfunctional band playing the soundtrack to your stress. But you, my friend, are the conductor. And it's time to change the tune.

Billy Mills: Defying the Architects to Claim Gold

Let's zoom in on a real-life legend: Billy Mills. This isn't just a guy who won a race; it's about how he tamed his dragons of negativity and mastered the trifecta of terrorizing voices—his Inner Voice, Ego, and the Human Collective—to become an Olympic champion. Many have forgotten Billy Mills, but his story is a powerful blueprint for defying what seems impossible.

Billy Mills' victory at the 1964 Tokyo Olympics was a stunning upset, making him the first, and still only, American to win gold in the 10,000-meter. It's a testament to raw inner resolve against overwhelming external and internal noise.

The Inner Voice: The Whispers of Inadequacy

Living under the weight of society's low expectations and his ego's yearning for proof, Mills undoubtedly battled a relentless Inner Voice. This saboteur might have hissed: "You're not good enough. They're right, you don't belong here." This voice amplified every past failure, every moment of doubt, and every cutting remark. It constantly tried to keep him "safe" by convincing him to just aim for a respectable finish, not a win.

This insidious voice could have sabotaged his focus, tightened his muscles, or made him question his training in the crucial moments. But Billy Mills fought back. He replaced that negative self-talk with empowering affirmations and tactical instructions. He famously wrote on a piece of paper: "I must believe I can run with the best in the world and win." This wasn't just optimism; it was a deliberate reprogramming of his internal narrative.

The Ego: The Desire for Recognition and the Sting of Doubt

The Ego craves acceptance and significance. Mills wanted to prove himself, not just to others, but to the self he saw in the mirror. The constant slights, the subtle racism, and the dismissive attitudes from competitors and media chipped at his confidence. His ego wrestled with the desire for external validation against the crushing weight of being overlooked, constantly being fed reasons to doubt its own worth.

He felt the immense pressure of representing his people, the yearning to prove everyone wrong, and the fear of letting himself and his community down. This intense internal pressure could have easily led to overthinking, tightening up, or collapsing.

But instead of letting his ego get caught up in proving others wrong or chasing fleeting approval, Mills channeled its energy into a higher purpose. His focus became about giving his absolute best effort, honoring his heritage, and discovering his own limits. He wasn't just running to win; he was running to execute his race plan perfectly and leave nothing on the track. This strategic shift moved his ego's focus from external validation to internal mastery.

The Human Collective: The Weight of Expectations and Racism

Billy Mills, an Oglala Lakota runner from humble beginnings, faced systemic racism and profound prejudice in 1960s America. The Human Collective—the dominant societal narrative—had already written his script. Coaches and others directly told him that as an "Indian," he could "run forever" but that "Negroes are sprinters," reflecting deeply ingrained stereotypes.

He endured a crushing moment when, after making the 1st Team Division 1 NCAA Cross Country All-American team, he was asked to step out of the team photo. These constant feelings of alienation and low self-esteem in a predominantly white world created an immense psychological barrier—a voice that constantly told him he didn't belong at that level, much less that he could ever win.

However, Mills found profound strength in the wisdom of his late father, who had told him as a grieving child, "now your wings are broken, but someday you'll have the wings of an eagle." This foundational message became a guiding voice, pushing him to pursue a dream as a means of healing. He famously wrote himself a goal: "Gold medal. Olympic 10,000-meter run." This wasn't just about winning a race; it was about healing a broken soul and reclaiming his narrative from the collective.

How Mills Silenced the Architects and Unleashed the Eagle

If you've never seen Mill's stunning win, it's worth a view on YouTube. World record holder Ron Clarke practically pushed him out of the race on the final lap. Mills says I wanted to fight, but I put all my effort into showing them I was a winner. In the final 100 meters, drawing on his redefined ego and his rejection of the Human Collective's narrative, he found a burst of energy, surged forward, and won by mere strides. It was less about physical superiority and more about an unshakeable belief in what he believed was possible, forged by silencing the inner demons.

Beyond his accomplishments on the track, Billy Mills remains a vibrant force for positive change. At the age of 87, he inspires audiences globally as a motivational speaker, promoting unity through diversity. He's the author of a children's book "Wings of an Eagle: The Gold Medal Dreams of Billy Mills". The ultimate testament to Billy Mills's enduring vision is the Dreamstarter program. Founded in 2015 under the umbrella of Running Strong for American Indian Youth, the program was created to directly empower Native youth. By providing them with a powerful combination of $20,000 grants and dedicated mentorship, Mills helps a new generation transform their own aspirations from a distant hope into a tangible reality.

Are you Doing Justice to Your Own Story?

Alright, magnificent human, let's talk about your story. We just watched Billy Mills look at the flimsy, prejudiced script the world handed him and basically say, "Nah, I'm writing my own Oscar-winning masterpiece." One that redeemed not just himself, but his entire lineage. But that kind of raw courage isn't exactly standard issue.

So, here's the gut-check question for you, right now: Are you actually happy with the story you're currently narrating about yourself? Or are you bored out of your mind with your own plot twists?

This is where my brilliant friend, Dr. Dennis Rebelo, comes in. His book, "Story Like You Mean It," isn't just some dusty tome on narrative theory; it's a power manual for unlocking your authentic voice and finally connecting with others on a profoundly human, no-BS level. Dennis, with his background spanning psychology, leadership, and communication, doesn't just teach you how to spin a yarn. Oh no, he digs deep into why it matters, and how to infuse every single word with genuine, soul-shaking meaning.

At its core, this book is about Unearthing Your Authentic Stories. And this isn't just for your key-locked diaries. This applies to everything. Dennis reveals the vital, transformative role authentic narrative plays in leadership, branding, and even kicking ass in business communication. He shows how leaders can wield their own genuine stories—and the raw, real stories of their organizations—to forge a powerful culture, ignite entire teams, and connect with customers on a level so deep, it feels like magic.

Just like the movie of your life, you can change the story you tell about yourself. From a flimsy, oh there's nothing much shoulder shrug, into a narrative that gets a standing ovation.

Unlocking Your Inner Oracle: My Wall Street Awakening

Wall Street, 1993. Forget what you think you know. This was the era of Jordan Belfort's audacious rise, George Soros's market-shaking maneuvers, and the lingering shadow of Michael Milken's once-unrivaled junk bond empire. And believe me, it was still a wild, unadulterated boys' club! Picture trading desks buzzing with frantic energy, bonuses so massive they could mortgage a yacht. And everyone, men and women, strutting in power suits that just squawked Master of the Universe!

Every morning I'd stride through the bustling World Trade Center–then a towering monument to raw ambition and unbridled power. Maybe it was that intense masculine energy and relentless drive that magnetically pulled me toward its absolute opposite: the mystical, mind-bending realm of metaphysics. Suddenly, I was neck-deep in studies you wouldn't expect from a Wall Streeter – Reiki, subliminal reprogramming, ancient spiritual disciplines. Every single one of them was geared toward one thing: cranking up self-mastery and supercharging higher awareness.

I was single, deep in the grind of my thirties, utterly immersed in that high-stakes, high-pressure world. But the truth is, I was already yearning for a path that offered something more than the relentless climb. I'd often blast mesmerizing Eastern-inspired soundscapes to transport me into a zone of meditation. And it was during one of these deep dives that something extraordinary happened: I heard a voice. Clear as a bell. It was female, incredibly wise, and radiated a kindness that instantly reminded me of my beloved grade school librarian.

Intrigued (and maybe a little freaked out), I mentioned this wild experience to my cousin, who just happens to be a Jungian therapist. Her question was simple: "Do you know who that voice is?" I paused, searching my gut, and then it dawned on me – a powerful realization that made my hair stand on end. The voice was me. But not the 'me' who battled the daily Wall Street chaos. This was a version of me that soared far beyond the rollercoaster of highs and lows. This was the Me I truly aspired to be, a self profoundly connected to a deeper wellspring of wisdom and unshakable peace.

In that moment, I realized something monumental: there was a space beyond the relentless noise. A powerful, quiet sanctuary beyond the prison of negativity and the suffocating grip of the collective. That experience wasn't just a turning point; it was a total paradigm shift. It solidified the understanding that within every single one of us lies an undeniable source of inner guidance, a wellspring of truth that just gets drowned out by the constant clamor of external consumption and that incessant internal ego chatter.

I had finally found a way to befriend my Higher Self. Not just befriend, but forge a divine connection, the ultimate antidote to those Architects of Anxiety. And this wasn't some fleeting whisper; it's a higher voice that has never left me. She's with me even when those thugs start barking their fear-mongering nonsense. And when I tune into her, I can finally escape those other gangsters.

I only discovered this powerful voice after fully immersing myself in the commitment to radical self-awareness and embracing absolutely all of who I was. Why? Because the most important relationship you will ever, ever have is the one with yourself. From the intoxicating first blush of new love to the profound depths of lasting connection you'll ever manifest in this life – they all pivot on your fearless commitment to truly knowing and boldly expressing your authentic, unvarnished self.

It's non-negotiable.

| Ready to invest in the most epic relationship of your life?

This is your Brain. This is your Brain on Drugs.

Remember that classic "This is your brain on drugs" commercial? You know, the one from 1987 with the sizzling egg? The whole point was to show how drugs can fry your brain. Confession: that ad always made me weirdly hungry!

But here's the kicker, and why it's actually brilliant: it was a clever, albeit dark, example of neuroplasticity in action. It showed how some things can seriously mess with your brain's wiring.

You see, our brains are not set in stone, not some rigid, unchanging lump. Your brain is flexible. Changeable. Literally plastic. The fancy term, "neuroplasticity," was actually cooked up by a Polish neuroscientist named Jerzy Konorski way back in 1948. But it took a while, a lot of hardcore research, for the scientific world to truly get hip to just how ridiculously amazing your brain's ability to reorganize itself by forming new connections throughout your entire life really is.

Today, neuroplasticity isn't just some fringe theory; it's a core truth in neuroscience. And research is constantly blowing our minds, revealing just how deep and wide this remarkable ability goes. Your brain isn't just reacting to life; it's actively rewriting its own script every single day. How cool is that?!

The Digital Circus of Modern Chaos

The modern world isn't a simple carousel; it's a deranged, multi-ring digital circus. The chaos is no longer just around you—it's piped directly into your pocket 24/7.

Social media is the dizzying ringmaster, demanding your attention with its endless, algorithmically perfected scroll. The 24/7 news cycle is the cannon-shooting daredevil, blasting you with "breaking alerts" that create immediate, high-stakes fear over global events and political crises you have zero control over. Politics is the tightrope clown act, teetering between outrage and absurdity, ensuring the entire collective audience is perpetually enraged and distracted. This overwhelming, manufactured pressure forces you to juggle the heavy load of your authentic Inner Voice against the demanding theatrics of your Ego shouting for external validation and the suffocating, cotton-candy-sweet pressure of the Human Collective. You're trying to find clarity while the relentless firehose of manufactured information bombards you like a rogue squirt gun. Seriously, it's enough to make my head spin, and I'm just words you're reading!

But all this delightful mayhem serves one vital purpose: to smack you upside the head with a truth so profound, it will literally set you free. Are you ready for it?

Your Thoughts Are Not You.

Let me say that again in a different way.

Your Thoughts Are Not TRUE.

Do you see it now? Do you see how all these sneaky constructs – these Architects of Anxiety – are absolutely hell-bent on keeping you exactly where you are? Stuck. Scared. Small.

But here's the glorious, liberating part: Others have broken free from this mental prison and you can too. It all boils down to one simple, powerful answer: You have the choice. You can consciously create new, kick-ass positive mental patterns to replace the old, crusty negativity holding you down.

Are you in?

The Runner's Brain: Forging New Pathways of Positivity & Longevity

Forget just "runner's high" – that's just the delicious appetizer. The real feast is the profound, lasting neurobiological transformation your brain undergoes with regular aerobic exercise. You're not just exercising your body; you're actively sculpting a more resilient, adaptable, and joyful mind.

Wiring Up Some Brain Bling – Neurogenesis & Synaptic Plasticity

Think of your brain as a vibrant garden. Running is like the ultimate gardening hack, making sure new growth sprouts and all the existing paths are clear and super-efficient.

- **Planting New Seeds**: Research, like that out of NYU Langone Health, shows that aerobic exercise (yes that means running!) actually stimulates the birth of new neurons in your hippocampus.

That's your brain's memory hub, responsible for learning and memory. You heard right: runners literally grow new brain cells!

- **Building Brain Autobahns**: Every time you hit the ground running, your brain isn't just counting steps; it's reinforcing the connections (synapses) between neurons. This is like upgrading those garden paths into multi-lane autobahns for lightning-fast communication, especially for motor control, coordination, and even sharp cognitive functions like focus and planning. You'll Danke me later.

- **The Runner's Edge**: Ever notice how a seasoned trail runner glides over roots and rocks without even thinking? That's not just muscle memory; it's strengthened neural pathways working their magic, allowing for incredibly fast, efficient communication between brain and body. Their brain built those superhighways!

Turning Your Brain into a Mental Ninja: Cognitive Superpowers

Beyond just feeling good, running actually makes you smarter. Seriously.

- **Level Up Your Brainpower**: Studies from the National Academy of Sciences prove it: regular running can dramatically improve your cognitive abilities. We're talking sharper attention span, laser-like concentration, and souped-up executive functions (like planning, decision-making, and getting your act together). This is all thanks to that increased blood flow, those brand-new brain cells, and those fortified neural connections.

- **The Runner's Flex**: A runner who mixes in some tough interval training isn't just boosting their fitness; they're training their brain to be a mental ninja. The demands of rapidly changing pace and intense bursts translate directly into improved mental sharpness and the ability to switch between tasks like a pro in other areas of life.

Running can literally increase your cognitive abilities and turn your brain into a powerhouse of clarity, memory, and razor-sharpness. Go on smarty-pants, give that brilliant brain the upgrade it deserves!

The Neurochemical Secret Sauce of Joy

Shall we talk about the delicious chemistry brewing in your brilliant brain, especially when you get that body moving? For years, everyone thought the "runner's high" was all about endorphins. And sure, endorphins are awesome natural painkillers your body pumps out. But here's the juicy scoop: most research now points to endocannabinoids as the true rockstars behind that blissful, calm, almost floating feeling you get after a good run.

Once this natural chemistry is unleashed, it contributes to:

- Reduced Pain Sensation: Your body's powerful natural relief system kicks in.

- Decreased Anxiety: That profound feeling of calm and ease that washes over you.

- Euphoria & Flow: A genuine sense of bliss and the effortless feeling of losing track of time.

Pretty cool, right? Your brain is literally rewarding you for putting in the effort. It's a built-in bliss button, primed to make you feel incredible just for moving your amazing self. No pharmacy required.

The Positive Path Framework: Brain Bliss for Everyone

I know you want these brain-boosting benefits! But you say, running just isn't my jam. No sweat (or maybe just a little!). The core principles behind how running rewires the brain can totally be applied to other activities. It's all about consistent, rhythmic movement that gently elevates your heart rate and engages your focus.

Here's your framework to get those brain cells firing, even if you'd rather binge-watch than jog:

1. Your Daily Dose of Delightful Movement

This is your non-negotiable foundation, your brain's happy hour! Think of it as your personal dance party, your daily dose of feel-good motion. What it means: you move your body every day.

- Your Brain's Playground: Forget the "hould" and find what makes you grin! We're talking brisk power walks, spontaneous dance-offs in your living room, hitting the cycling class with wild abandon, splashing around in the pool like a mermaid, getting your fierce on with kickboxing, conquering a scenic hike, or even just jamming out on the elliptical or rowing machine.

- Why It Works: No matter your jam, these activities consistently get your heart pumping and blood flowing to that brilliant brain. That's the secret sauce for cranking up BDNF production and literally growing those shiny new brain cells!

- Action Plan: Find something you actually enjoy and make it a non-negotiable appointment with your brilliant self. Mix it up to keep it fun!

2. Turn Your Workout into a Brain-Soothing Meditation!

This is where your movement becomes pure magic for your mind! Think of that "in the zone" feeling – where your body just flows, and your mind feels crystal clear, totally receptive, and utterly chill.

- Your Brain's Zen Mode: When you truly engage with every glorious move and ditch the distractions, you're rolling out the red carpet for those soothing Alpha and Theta brainwaves. This isn't just about feeling good; it literally quiets that noisy Inner Voice, supercharges your creativity, and wraps you in a blanket of deep relaxation.

- Action Plan: Seriously, put that phone away. Focus on your breath, the rhythm of your movement, the delicious sensations in your body. If your mind decides to wander off to Tahiti, gently lasso it back. And pick music that makes you feel like a total boss, not something that'll send you down a rabbit hole of distractions!

3. Keep Your Brain Guessing – and Growing

Your brain is no couch potato, it loves a good challenge! This isn't about crushing yourself; it's about giving your eager mind new puzzles to solve and new ways to sparkle.

- Your Brain's Thrill Ride: This means gradually upping the ante on your workouts – whether it's going a little longer, pushing a bit harder, or trying something completely new.

- Why It Works: Your brain literally thrives on novelty! Learning new movements or gently nudging yourself beyond your comfort zone isn't just for your muscles; it actively stimulates brand-new neural connections and strengthens the ones you've already got. This keeps your brain razor-sharp, adaptable, and perpetually ready for anything.

- Action Plan: Ditch the rut! Don't do the exact same workout every single time. Sign up for that funky new dance class, explore a totally different walking trail, try a new swimming stroke, or crank up the resistance on your bike. Ever thought about pickleball or tennis? Give your brain some exciting new problems to solve!

Bonus – The Neuroplasticity Nightclub: Ditch the dull routine—if you want the ultimate brain boost, you need to hit the dance floor! Why do experts call Dancing the best workout for your gray matter? Because it uniquely forces your brain to do three things at once: track physical movement, access memory for steps, and constantly adapt to new rhythms or partners. This fierce combination of aerobic energy and intense cognitive activity is the neuroscientist's jackpot!

4. Strategic Recovery & Fueling: Your Brain's Spa Day

Listen up, because this part is crucial! All that amazing brain-building you're doing? Those new, precious brain cells need some serious pampering to truly stick around and thrive. Think of it as giving your brain a luxurious spa day.

- Your Brain's Chill-Out Time: This means honoring your rest days like they're sacred holidays! And when it comes to grub, it's all about fueling your sweet body with love, not just stuffing your gourd with whatever's handy. It's about giving your brilliant self the adequate sleep it needs for a full-on repair and rebuild.

- Why It Works: Those shiny new brain cells you're growing? They're delicate little superstars! They absolutely need proper rest and all the right nutrients to seamlessly integrate into your vast, magnificent neural networks. Without it, they're just… chilling without a purpose.

- Action Plan: Seriously, prioritize 7-9 hours of quality sleep every single night. No excuses! Hydrate like it's your full-time job. And when it comes to food, become a brain-food connoisseur: load up on healthy fats (hello, avocados!), grab that lean protein, and feast on vibrant fruits and veggies like they're going out of style. Give your brain the VIP treatment it deserves.

You don't need to be chasing a marathon medal to build a better brain. Not even close. You just need to commit to moving your body consistently, mindfully, and progressively. That's it! Your brain is practically vibrating, ready to get rewired for more health, more happiness, and a whole lot more awesome years ahead!

Ready to get moving and grow that brilliant mind?

Rules of the Road

- Here's the Finisher Medal for Exploring the Scary Voice in Your Head

- You learned about the Architects of Anxiety: The Inner Voice, EGO & Human Collective

- But there's hope because the brain is plastic and it's yours to change for the better

- How runners rewire new pathways for health, positivity, & longevity

- You got your very own Brain Bliss Workout Plan

Ready to crash the Neuroplasticity Nightclub?

Shall we keep Jogging?

CHAPTER 5

BE AN OWNER, NOT A CONSUMER

Remember Black Friday, 2011? Most folks recall the online sales surge – a tidy 11% jump – and the usual Christmas shopping frenzy. But beneath that sparkly trend, something far more disturbing was boiling over. That year, Black Friday wasn't just about discounted flat-screens; it devolved into a full-blown chaotic melee. We're talking brawls, gunfire, trampling, pepper spray, stun guns, an armed robbery attempt, and even a fight over jewelry at Walmart. People were literally throwing down over trinkets. Talk about a reality check!

And while that wild display of consumer frenzy was playing out, something truly extraordinary happened. Yvon Chouinard, the visionary genius behind Patagonia, the outdoor clothing company, dropped a full-page ad in The New York Times. And what did it say? Splashed starkly across one of their iconic jackets were four words that slapped you awake:

"Don't Buy This Jacket"

Let that sink in for a sizzling second. A half billion-dollar company, on the biggest shopping day of the year, actively telling you to NOT buy their stuff. This wasn't some sneaky marketing trick designed to get you to buy more. Oh no, my shopaholic. This was a profoundly powerful statement about conscious consumption about the true, gnarly impact of our choices and ultimately about true ownership.

Chouinard's an iconoclast for a reason. He's a mountain man, an environmental activist, and a successful author who built Patagonia on principles that blow past quarterly profits. He's living proof you can build a global enterprise with a conscience, while staying fiercely committed to your planet and your people. His message wasn't just about a jacket; it was a wake-up call to look beyond immediate desire and really consider the ripple effect of our actions. It was a stark reminder that true ownership isn't about accumulating more; it's about making deliberate, mindful choices in every aspect of your life. He basically called out society's "buy it, trash it" mentality.

That single ad, my spelunker, encapsulates a profound shift we all need to make in our lives – a shift that's just as crucial for cultivating a Marathon Mindset as logging those long miles. It's the move from being a passive consumer to an active owner.

The Planet's Power Play: Owning Our Resources

For those of you who actually give a damn about this little 'ole blue planet, there's a game-changing philosophy that's gaining serious, undeniable traction. It's called the Circular Economy, and it's basically the ultimate power move for our precious resources. Think of it as the universe's biggest, most epic glow-up!

Let's rewind a bit, back to the Industrial Revolution. Amazing leap forward, right? Designed to make life "easier" with incredible new machines, mass production, bustling factories, and a whole new influx of jobs. For a while, it totally seemed like magic! Suddenly, stuff was cheaper, more accessible, and life was just getting "better."

But here's the dirty secret, the one they didn't put on the brochures: this "easier" life came with a massive, hidden cost. The Industrial Revolution basically hardwired us into what we now call the Linear Economy. It's the ultimate "take, make, dispose" trap, and let me tell you, it's been draining our planet dry like a milkshake with a hole in the bottom.

Think about it. We started taking raw materials from the Earth at an unprecedented, frantic pace – digging up minerals like they were free candy, chopping down forests like they were weeds, and sucking up fossil fuels like there was an endless supply. Spoiler alert: there isn't!

Then, we'd make products like crazy, often with absolutely zero thought for what happened once they were "done." We even invented "planned obsolescence" – a sneaky little trick where products were designed to break or become outdated quickly, just so you'd have to buy a new one!

We're talking about those infamous lightbulb manufacturers, the auto industry's annual "new look" shenanigans, those "indestructible" nylon stockings that suddenly weren't, and all those digital dongles and weird connectors that magically stopped working with your slightly older stuff.

You'd use your shiny new thingie for a bit, maybe even love it. And then, because it was cheaper to replace or literally designed to fail, you'd just dispose of it. Straight to the landfill.

The Clean-up Act

But here's the good news, we're finally putting policies into play that kick that linear way of thinking to the curb. It's called Circular Economy. This philosophy is all about owning what we consume by designing waste OUT of the system from the absolute beginning. Instead of that one-way street to the landfill, it's about creating a closed loop where every single resource is kept in play for as long as humanly possible. It's built on core principles, all driven by seriously smart design, turning trash into treasure and problems into possibilities:

- Eliminate Waste and Pollution: This means we're getting super strategic, designing products and systems so that waste and pollution are never created in the first place. Think about packaging that's so clean it could practically dissolve into thin air, or products made from non-toxic, endlessly recyclable materials. It's about being proactive, not just cleaning up someone else's mess!

- Circulate Products and Materials: This is where you become a total rockstar of resourcefulness! It's all about keeping products and their valuable components in the economy, at their highest value, for as long as humanly possible.

This includes:

- **Reuse:** This is all about getting creative and finding new ways to love your stuff! Think refilling that coffee mug Aunt Edna gave you at Christmas, instead of grabbing a paper cup.

- **Repair:** Got a broken toaster? A ripped pair of jeans? Instead of tossing it, you fix it! This is about taking back control and saying "no" to the throwaway culture. You're empowered to make things last.

- **Refurbish/Remanufacture:** Get your McGuyver on! Bring old products back to "as new" condition or using their parts to make new ones.

- **Recycle:** As a last resort, breaking down materials to create new products when something truly can't be reused, repaired, or remanufactured, do we break it down to its core materials to create something totally new. It's the ultimate transformation, keeping those precious resources in play.

The Circular Economy is your invitation to become an owner of our collective future. It's about recognizing that every choice we make about what we buy, use, and discard has a ripple effect. Can we ditch the "trash" mindset and embrace a world where everything has value, and nothing is truly wasted? Let's make this planet thrive, shall we?

Brand Leaders: Owning the Revolution

These companies are translating their ethos into tangible results, proving you can build a thriving business while making the Earth proud. Take a page from their book about owning our resources and our impact.

Fairphone – Tech Rebels

In an industry notorious for planned obsolescence, Fairphone flips the script. They design phones that are shockingly easy to repair – buy individual components and swap them yourself! This modular magic, plus up to 8 years of software support, puts longevity in your hands. Beyond repair, Fairphone owns ethical sourcing, ensuring fair labor and responsible mining for materials like gold and cobalt, even running e-waste recycling programs in places like Ghana.

REI: Adventures in Sustainability

Outdoor enthusiasts know lasting value, and REI embodies it. Their #OptOutside campaign encourages ditching Black Friday shopping for nature. Their real circular superpower is the robust REI Used Gear program, where you buy and sell pre-owned items, giving gear a second life and keeping it out of landfills. They also champion repair and longevity with extensive guides and in-store experts, proving that making products last is the best way to reduce environmental impact.

Nudie Jeans: Denim That Lives Forever

While fast fashion churns out waste, Nudie Jeans is a shining example of circularity in clothing. Their absolute mic-drop moment? Free repairs for life on all their jeans! They want you to wear them until they fall apart, not toss them. Beyond repairs, their re-use program offers a 20% discount on new jeans when you bring back old ones, which are then restored for resale or recycled into new products. They're committed to 100% organic cotton and constant sustainable innovation, truly owning the full loop.

Temptation Island: When Your Wallet Goes Rogue

Alright, let's talk about the Shopping Temptation, because it's a sneaky little beast that turns even the most iron-willed among us into impulse-buying zombies.

Ever notice how you end up with stuff you never even wanted in the first place? Like, how did that avocado slicer suddenly leap into your cart when you just wanted cat food? That, my friend, is no accident. It's because marketers are absolute geniuses at using their algorithms to practically read your mind (and your wallet!).

They're constantly serving you personalized product recommendations based on all your digital breadcrumbs: what you've clicked, what you've browsed, what you've bought, even how long you hovered over that ridiculous inflatable flamingo. Sites like Amazon, Etsy, Target, Shein, and every online shop in between are locked and loaded, always showing you:

- **Recommended for You**. Translation: *We know what you secretly desire!*

- **Customers Who Bought This Also Bought**. Translation: *Peer pressure, online style!*

- **Recently Viewed Items**. Translation: *Still thinking about that flamingo, aren't you?*

It's a carefully crafted digital lure, designed to make you feel like you need something you didn't even know existed five minutes ago. Your job, my precious addict, is to recognize the trap, before your credit card has a meltdown. Knowing this is the first step to becoming an Owner of what you consume, not just a passive recipient.

Take it from Sy Syms, founder of the New York City clothing store chain SYMS, and his famous marketing slogan: "An Educated Consumer is Our Best Customer".

Become the CSI of Your Mind

In this hyper-connected, often overwhelming world, you simply cannot passively assume that everything you're exposed to is real or true. Information is just raw data; it doesn't automatically equate to genuine knowledge, or most importantly, Truth.

That puts YOU in the driver's seat to sort through all the input. To make judgment calls on what you watch, listen to, and engage your precious emotions with. You have to develop a discerning eye. You have to question sources. You need to actively seek multiple perspectives. Be an active investigator of the information landscape, my friends, not a passive recipient.

So, what's the answer? How do you protect your mind in a world economy explicitly designed to keep you glued and consuming? It comes down to you. It's your responsibility to step out of the current, to take the reins. It's about taking ownership of what you allow into every single aspect of your life – your home, your family, your body, and most importantly, your mind.

The Solution: Be an Owner, Not a Consumer

You take ownership every day. It's in the small, powerful choices.

- Choosing quality fuel for your body instead of that greasy fast-food sprint.

- Seizing your morning with purpose, instead of letting your phone's dings dictate your day.

- Crafting your own coffee (customized with lion's mane, creatine or collagen), rather than hitting the drive-thru on autopilot.

- Fixing that slightly broken lamp or mending those favorite jeans, instead of a mindless "add to cart" click.

- Diving into connection with a real flesh and blood person, ditching the endless scroll through everyone else's highlight reels.

- Reclaiming your mental space by silencing notifications, refusing to let every ping hijack your attention.

Own Your Power

Let's cut to the chase, because when I'm teaching Leadership classes at colleges, there's one vital rule I always hammer home. It's a truth that cuts through all the noise, all the excuses, all the "woe is me" stories: Nobody else is responsible for creating the life you truly desire. Not your parents, not your spouse, not your minister, rabbi, priest, or even your favorite elastic yoga instructor.

So, I ask them, and I'm asking you right now:

> Are you the person you've always wanted to become? If not, then why the hell not?

Whose permission are you waiting for to live the life of your dreams? Who needs to give you the green light to feel healthier, to be happier, more loved, to pursue that audacious, terrifying, exhilarating goal?

This brings us right back to that idea of ownership, and it connects directly to this universal, undeniable law of achievement and success. And who better to articulate it than Brian Tracy himself – seriously, he's like the Yoda of sales and professional development!

According to Tracy, you are 100% fully responsible for everything you are, everything you have, and everything you become. There's no wiggling out of that, no passing the buck. But here's the kicker, and this is the part that's truly liberating: it's not a burden, my friend. It's a profoundly powerful, incredibly freeing realization. Because when you own all of it, you also own all the power to change it.

Permission to Run: The Mind's True Marathon

And speaking of profound, liberating realizations, let me introduce you to a runner who absolutely embodied that true Owner spirit. This isn't about fast legs and mileage; it's about mastery of the mind.

> *"Don't be concerned if running or exercise will add years to your life; be concerned with adding life to your years."*
>
> *– George Sheehan*

George Sheehan wrote himself the ultimate permission slip to run, not just as a physical act, but as a path to a richer, more authentic life. You see, George was a successful cardiologist, living what most people would consider a pretty good life. But deep down, in his mid-40s, he hit a wall. As the text says, he was "restless, bored, and feeling a bit 'fat in his body, fat in his brain, and fat in his soul.'" Oof, we've all been there, right?

So, what did Doc Sheehan do? He didn't wait for a doctor's orders (he was the doctor!). He didn't wait for a new fad diet or a self-help guru. He simply laced up his shoes and started running. Now, this wasn't about winning races or hitting some arbitrary fitness goal, at least not initially. This was about a profound act of self-permission. He gave himself permission to:

Prioritize inner fulfillment over external expectations: As a cardiologist, perhaps society expected him to focus on traditional markers of success. But he was feeling empty. His decision to run was a radical shift, an internal declaration that his own sense of aliveness and joy was paramount.

Embrace discomfort for growth: Running, especially when you're starting later in life and feeling "fat in your body," isn't easy. It's uncomfortable, it's challenging. But he gave himself permission to lean into that discomfort because he intuitively knew it would lead to something deeper.

Use running as a "laboratory" for self-discovery: He didn't just run miles; he ran into himself. The roads became his personal space to explore his "courage, his limits, and his capacity for joy and endurance." He gave himself permission to be both the scientist and the subject in his own grand experiment of living fully.

In essence, George Sheehan looked at his life, recognized what was missing, and instead of waiting for someone else to fix it or give him a roadmap, he gave himself permission to embark on a deeply personal journey. Sheehan taught us that running isn't just about covering distance; it's about uncovering yourself. It's a laboratory where you learn about your courage, your limits, and your capacity for joy and endurance.

Locus of Control: Who's Driving Your Bus?

Let's get to the heart of what it means to be an Owner of your own life. We're talking about your Locus of Control – basically, where you believe the power lies when things happen to you. Is it all on you confidently navigating the turns, Inner Locus of Control? Or is the universe messing with you so that you feel like you're just a passenger, along for the ride, at the mercy of every pothole and detour, External Locus of Control.

This isn't about right or wrong answers, just about getting real with yourself. Read each statement and decide if it sounds more like something YOU believe (meaning, you're the boss) or if it sounds like something "The Universe," "Luck," or "Other People" are in charge of.

Ready? Let's roll!

Your Locus of Control Power Quiz!

Pick the statement that resonates most with you. Don't forget to write down your answers so you can tally them at the end.

Be introspective. Have fun.

1. When something good happens to me...

    A. It's usually because I worked hard and made it happen. (You'r Awesome!)

    B. I was just lucky, or the stars aligned perfectly. (The Universe's Whim!)

2. If I don't get a promotion or a raise...

    A. I need to look at what I can do differently to improve my skills or approach. (My Next Move!)

    B. My boss clearly plays favorites, or the company just isn't fair. (Blame Game!)

3. When I have an argument with someone...

   A. I usually consider what role my words or actions played. (My Part!)

   B. They just don't listen, or they're being totally unreasonable. (Their Fault!)

4. To stay healthy and fit...

   A. It's all about my consistent choices in diet and exercise. (My Daily Hustle!)

   B. It mostly depends on my genes or whether I get sick. (Genetic Lottery!)

5. When I'm facing a big challenge...

   A. I believe my effort and determination will get me through it. (My Grit!)

   B. Some problems are just too big, and there's not much I can do. (Destiny's Call!)

6. If I feel anxious or stressed...

   A. I can use my tools (like meditation or exercise) to shift my mindset. (My Inner Toolkit!)

   B. It's just how I'm wired, or it's because of all the crazy stuff happening around me. (External Overload!)

7. When I look at my future...

   A. I feel excited to design and create the life I want. (My Masterpiece!)

   B. I hope things work out, but it's hard to predict what will happen. (Fingers Crossed!)

Drumroll, Please! Your Locus of Control Reveal!

Count up how many "A" answers you chose and how many "B" answers.

Mostly "A" Answers? You, my friend, have a strong **Internal Locus of Control**! You believe you're the powerful director of your own life's movie. You take responsibility, you're proactive, and you know your actions directly influence your outcomes. You're a true owner, not just a consumer of life! Keep rocking that empowered mindset!

Mostly "B" Answers? It sounds like you might lean towards an **External Locus of Control**. You might feel that outside forces, luck, or other people have more say in your destiny. But here's the good news: awareness is the first step to change! You have the power to start taking the reins. It's time to realize you have more control than you think – and you can absolutely start directing your own blockbuster!

A Mix of A's and B's? Welcome to the **wonderfully human middle**! Most of us have a blend. You probably recognize your own agency in some areas of life, while feeling a bit more at the mercy of external forces in others. The key is to notice where you're giving away your power and start flexing that internal muscle. You're a work in progress, and that's perfectly awesome!

No matter your score, remember this: understanding your Locus of Control is a huge step toward creating the life you truly desire. Are you ready to grab that steering wheel?

Locus of Control – Trail Edition

My husband Wayne still jokes that my early races were less about running and more about a full-blown competition with Mother Nature. And he's not entirely wrong.

See, I knew how to control my life. I was the driver of my own 5-speed manual Porsche – full throttle, totally in charge! But when it came to the trails, to those wild, unpredictable races, I wasn't quite ready to admit that the elements might have their own agenda. So, in Wayne's words, I'd unconsciously "create bizarre obstacles" on the road. You know, just to challenge nature's locus of control.

Like the time we hit the Breckenridge Crest Half Marathon. Oh, it was a warm, sunny day in early September when we started, so naturally, I left our winter gear chilling in the car. BIG MISTAKE. The first half of that race is all incline, starting from a breezy 9,600 feet. Then, at 4.5 miles, it just starts taking a steep, brutal elevation until you hit the peak at a lung-busting 12,534 feet.

As we were climbing, it started to snow. Just a few flakes at first, pretty and innocent. But then, it came down in earnest. By the time we actually reached the peak, it was a full-blown blizzard! And remember our gear?

Yeah, we were rocking shorts and short-sleeved tops. I was shivering so hard, my hands swelled up like balloons – I could barely even close them! I had to literally beg one of the trail crew helpers to open my gel pack for me. And the breathing? Forget about it. Slow, labored, every single step felt like a giant vice was squishing my chest. That was a serious "external locus" smackdown! But then, once we finally crested that beast, it was all downhill, and suddenly, I could run again. The finish line was pure bliss: sunshine, smiles, and well-earned Tequila shots. Wayne, ever the understated one, just shook his head. "Weather can be unpredictable," he mumbled, "but I've never seen a blizzard quite like that."

And then there was the time we were hiking the Mist Trails at Yosemite. Seven glorious miles out and back, starting from the iconic John Muir Trail itself. It's a glorious climb, all rocky switchbacks and that famous, giant staircase carved right into the cliffside. Every step a testament to nature's raw power and the hardy souls who cherish natural beauty. Breathtaking vistas of Half Dome towering like a granite god, the valley floor stretching out below, and those crazy hikers sliding down the rocks at Vernal Falls and Nevada Falls to bathe in the icy spray.

We were already buzzing from our wildlife sightings that trip – graceful Mule deer grazing in sun-dappled clearings, plump sassy marmots sunbathing on warm rocks, and the majestic, circling red-tailed hawks, masters of the thermals. But, I have to admit, a little part of me was still secretly forlorn that I hadn't yet spotted a rattlesnake. Just a glimpse, you know?

We descended along outcropping boulders, each one a miniature ecosystem, festooned with emerald mosses and alpine shrubs – perhaps a tenacious Sierra juniper clinging to the granite, or the last stubborn bloom of a delicate columbine, defying the thin air. Water trickled down like a tranquility garden. It felt like walking through one of Muir's own sermons, a living cathedral of stone and hardy flora, where every plant seemed to whisper tales of endurance.

Then, while running back, as the late-day sun painted the canyon walls gold, we came across a Northern Pacific Rattlesnake. Just chilling there, coiled perfectly, soaking up the last warm rays, a silent, ancient guardian of the trail, perhaps a spirit of the rocks itself. We gingerly stepped past it. "REALLY?!" Wayne yelled, throwing his hands up, his voice echoing a bit too loudly for the serene moment. "I can't believe you conjured a snake!"

To this day, before any big race, Wayne will look at me with that knowing smirk and ask, "So, are we planning an earthquake this time? Or maybe a volcano eruption?" And you know what? I've finally learned to laugh with him. Because I've embraced the profound truth: I don't and can't control everything.

Instead of fighting the elements, I've learned to trust. To trust that the path ahead, even with its unexpected elements or obstacles, will be fun, rewarding, and ultimately safe. This isn't surrender; it's liberation. That deep, unwavering trust is precisely what transforms potential calamity into exhilarating adventure. Because when it comes down to it, Mother Nature is the ultimate magnificent Race Director. And I'm here for every wild, beautiful mile she throws my way.

The Ultimate Act of Ownership: Reclaim Your Brain

Alright, there's one more mega important element to this whole Ownership thing that we all need to nail.

Does this ever happen to you? You're cruising along, being you, and then BAM! You hear or see some news report, some rant, some "expert" spouting off a narrative that absolutely revolts you. You despise the message, you can't stand the person delivering it, and you'd rather gnaw off your pinkie finger than listen for one more second.

But it's too late, isn't it? It's already in your head. And it's tunneled like that creepy Ceti eel from Star Trek – the one that burrows into your ear, clamps onto your cerebral cortex, and makes you totally susceptible to outside suggestion. And then madness, and eventual death. Trekkies out there know!

Dueling Anchors

And as that unwanted thought continues to worm its way into your brilliant mind – precisely because you hate it with so much fiery passion – you jump into the internal debate. "NO!" you furiously dispute, "there's this and this and that!" Pretty soon, you've got dueling anchors or talk show hosts playing full-blast in your head, and guess what? You're one of them! You're coiffed, in a snappy blue jacket, passionately stating your opinions in a head-to-head battle with a voice you despise.

I used to do this ALL. THE. TIME. I'd get totally sucked into those screaming news flashes, those "urgent" reports, those wild opinions from people I'd never even have coffee with, much less respect. And let me tell you, it tore me apart. It absolutely consumed me – devoured my time, zapped my energy, and shattered my hard-earned peace of mind.

Then, it hit me like a lightning bolt: Wait a minute. What I'm really doing here is allowing the voices of others to torment me. To sabotage my serenity. To keep me captive in this endless loop of collective consciousness, which is often a swirling cesspool of fear, loss of control, hopelessness, and powerlessness.

And that's when I had the ultimate realization:

| YOU CAN'T USE MY HEAD FOR YOUR PLATFORM!

This, my friend, is the ultimate frontier of ownership. It's about drawing a fierce boundary around your mental space. Your brain isn't a public billboard for every random rant or fear-mongering narrative out there. It's your sacred creative space, your inner sanctuary. You get to decide who and what gets airtime.

Your Eyesballs are the ROI

Your attention isn't just valuable; it's untarnished gold! As a marketing executive, I can tell you straight up: engagement is the most valuable currency in the entire digital world.

Companies aren't just slapping up a few ads and hoping for a quick click. Oh no. They're furiously, strategically fighting for your attention because your eyeballs are the ultimate ROI (that's "Return On Investment" for those not fluent in biz-speak).

They're using every platform, every algorithm, every calculated trick in the book to:

- Build Relationships: Make you feel like you know them, like you're part of their tribe.
- Shape Perceptions: Get you to think a certain way about their brand, their product, or even a political idea.

- Drive Specific Objectives: Whether it's to boost brand awareness, generate leads, rack up sales, or subtly influence your vote, your gaze is their gold.

Your attention isn't just something you give away; it's being fiercely competed for. Understanding this is the first step to becoming an owner of your own focus!

The AI Takeover: They Know You Better Than You Know Yourself

Here's where it gets wild: You're watching a video, just minding your own business, and all of a sudden, Oprah pops up selling pink salt. "Wow," you think, "that's weird. But it has to be real, it's Oprah!" Guess what? It's almost certainly AI-generated, beamed straight into your feed. This isn't science fiction, it's reality. These "deepfake" ads leverage your trust to trick you. The voice might sound slightly off, the lip sync might be a bit out, or the claims are just too good to be true.

This AI surge is massive:

- The Bot Backbone: On average, nearly 50% of all internet traffic is non-human, generated by automated bots (Imperva Bot Traffic Report, 2024). This isn't just about ads; it's about news, reviews, and political narratives. This constant stream of automated activity contributes significantly to the noise, making authentic human voices harder to find.

- Deepfake Reality: The number of deepfake videos and audio clips is rising alarmingly fast. Reports show a year-over-year increase of over 400% in malicious deepfakes detected globally, primarily targeting financial fraud and political manipulation (Sensity AI/ Resecurity Annual Report, 2024).

- Synthetic Surge: The global volume of synthetic media (AI-generated text, images, and video) is growing exponentially. Some analysts project that over 99% of images viewed online could be AI-generated by 2030 (Future of Content Report, 2023).

- Advertising Overload: The volume of AI-optimized, hyper-personalized advertising content being pumped into user feeds (like the pink salt' example) has increased by over 70% in the last two years, utilizing AI to bypass human skepticism (eMarketer Digital Ad Spend Report, 2024).

This isn't just a future problem; it's a tidal wave that's already here.

The true depth of this takeover is the constant data feedback loop. Every scroll, every hesitation, every moment you stare a little too long at a photo of your ex's new life, or a news headline that triggers your anxiety—all of it is data. This data is fed instantly back into the AI, allowing it to construct a shockingly accurate, continuously updated model of your personality, insecurities, political leanings, and impulse buy triggers. The AI doesn't just guess what you want; it knows what specific, emotional stimuli are required to make you stop, click, and override your rational brain to perform an immediate action.

The Attention War and the Owner's Mindset

This brings us to the core problem of the modern attention economy: You are not fighting a fair fight. This is not a battle of simple willpower between you and a benign device; it's a fight against a billion-dollar machine optimized by the world's best data scientists and behavioral psychologists. Their sole KPI is to optimize for your attention and consumption, not your well-being, your focus, or your ability to achieve long-term goals like overcoming negativity.

If the technological environment is designed to be manipulative, addictive, and constantly rewarding the immediate, then individual discipline alone will fail. The only effective defense against this digital onslaught is to shift your mindset entirely: Stop being a passive consumer and start being an intentional owner of your attention, your data, and your time. Becoming an owner means understanding the machine, dismantling its hooks, and demanding a fundamental redesign of the very products that have hijacked your attention.

The Resistance: The Center for Humane Technology

This critical work of reclaiming human agency—of turning consumption back into ownership—is where we turn next, specifically to the advocacy and solutions proposed by the Center for Human Technology.

This isn't just a grassroots rebellion; it's a powerful force of fighting this battle at the highest level. I'm talking about the Center for Humane Technology. Their message is simple but profound: technology is in a race for the bottom of the brainstem, and we're losing.

They're not just complaining about the problem; they're taking action. They are on the front lines, sounding the alarm on AI's potential to turbocharge misinformation, polarization and social despair on a scale we've never seen before. They're pushing for a new regulatory framework, challenging the very business models that profit from your addiction. They're working to build a "humane AI" that aligns with human well-being, not just corporate profit. They're advocating for a world where technology serves us, rather than the other way around.

By simplifying the complex, humanizing the technical, and providing a clear framework for action, CHT empowers non-experts to understand the existential nature of AI and encourage the necessary steps to govern it. They serve as a crucial bridge, translating the code of tomorrow into the policy of today.

Their fight is an incredible example of collective ownership, but it all comes back to you. They can push for the new rules, but you must fight the battle in your own mind.

Why Being an Owner is Non-Negotiable

Let's connect these dots, because understanding how you are being targeted, used and cajoled into the group mindset of despair and powerlessness is precisely why being an Owner of your movie – and especially your mind – isn't just a good idea, it's your absolute secret weapon.

Here's why taking ownership is your ultimate superpower against the digital deluge:

You Own Your Filter–No Algorithm Required: Media, newsfeeds, and AI are all clever little puppet masters, designed solely to hook you and keep you scrolling 'til your thumb cramps. But you, my friend, are the Owner of your own mental VIP list. You get to decide what gets in, what truly fuels your spirit, and what gets sent straight to the spam folder, instead of letting some algorithm guess what you actually want to click on.

You Own Your Truth–No Synthetic Stories Here: When the internet's flooding with AI-generated everything alongside biased news and sensational headlines, the lines between real and ridiculously fake get blurrier than a drunk selfie. A true Owner isn't just passively chugging down whatever narrative the media, AI, or your newsfeed is serving up. You're a fierce, critical thinker, questioning the source, sniffing out the fakery, and forming your own brilliant beliefs. Your truth is yours, period.

You Own Your Creativity–Time to Make Your Own Damn Magic: Sure, it's easy to just binge-watch endless streams of AI-created content, scroll through curated newsfeeds, or consume everyone else's opinions. You could practically drown in it! But a real Owner isn't just a consumer of other people's (or robot's) genius. You're prioritizing making your own stuff, sharing your unique voice, and stamping your original, undeniable mark on this wild world.

You Own Your Time & Attention–Your Most Precious Assets: The entire digital universe is dedicated to one thing: snagging your eyeballs and holding them hostage. But an Owner guards their time and attention like it's solid gold. Because it is. You consciously decide where to invest your focus, shutting down those sneaky engagement traps and pouring your energy into what truly builds your life, instead of just zapping your brain cells.

In an age where algorithms and endless content streams increasingly shape our digital world, ownership is your rebellion. It's your declaration that your mind, your time, and your values are too precious to be passively consumed by external forces. It's how you stay sane, stay powerful, and truly live your own incredible life amidst the digital wild west.

Great Question to ask #3:

| What Do They Know That I Don't?

The Christmas Card Revelation: Eyes That Stopped Me Cold

Okay, so every year, I'm on a mission: the annual family Christmas card. And since Wayne's about as eager to say 'cheese' as a vampire watching the sun rise, our dogs usually get to be the stars. It's always a riot sifting through all the cherished montages and chronicles from real families.

One year, I was clicking through templates on Shutterfly, and whoa! There she was. This woman, probably in her 60s, with a gorgeous cascade of white hair wearing a flowy blue top, surrounded by her dashing husband and grown kids. Great family portrait!

But what really snagged my attention were her eyes. They weren't just pretty; they were radiating this utterly blissful, serene happiness. And my immediate thought was *This Woman Has Lived a Really Happy Life.*

Now, I'm not naive. I'm sure she'd weathered her fair share of grief, disappointment, and flat-out life curveballs. Given her age, she absolutely had to have gone through a ton of stuff the universe threw her way. But despite all that, her eyes held this incredible look of tranquility and peace.

So, of course, my brain went straight to the big question: What does she know that I don't? What's the secret to a peace so tranquil, a joy so radiant, that it actually stops people–like me–dead in their tracks?

And if I'm not mistaken, you would too.

It boils down to one glorious, life-changing word: Freedom.

Freedom to be exactly who you are. Freedom to think what you want. Freedom for your magnificent mind to be a safe, sacred place. But here's the kicker: it doesn't just happen. You don't just poof into it.

- You have to choose it.
- You have to commit to the new program freaking every single day.

We already talked about some hard-hitting truths, didn't we? That nagging voice in your head? It isn't YOU. And it isn't TRUE. You have to dig in your heels and vow: *"Yo inner critic, you have nothing to do with my life!"* And in truth, it doesn't. When you're fiercely choosing happiness and peace, all those other soapboxes can't even dent your incredible life.

You created the life you're living, after all! You chose the partner, the dog (and those two cats!). You picked the cute apartment near the park, Wegmans and TJ Maxx. Close to that adorable Peruvian restaurant with the garden patio.

Why then would You allow ANYbody to steal your Joy?

The Inner & Outer Game of Ownership

Notice a trend here? First, you quiet that inner voice. The next logical, glorious step is to quiet the external voices. This is where the wisdom of Don Miguel Ruiz drops in like a perfectly timed water station during a marathon.

His book "The Voice of Knowledge" aligns perfectly with being an Owner instead of a Consumer. Ruiz, that brilliant Toltec spiritual teacher, nails it: so much of our suffering comes from believing the lies – about ourselves, about the world – we've swallowed since we were wee babies. These lies become that annoying "Voice of Knowledge" constantly chattering in our minds, undermining our true potential and joy.

Ruiz's work is a game-changer for true ownership. It teaches us that the greatest act of power is taking charge of our own internal world – the thoughts we entertain, the beliefs we hold about ourselves, the stories we tell. When you silence that damaging "Voice of Knowledge" and reconnect with your inner integrity, you unlock the profound power to create your own reality, find your purpose, and jog straight back to your true, unburdened self. It's the ultimate internal marathon, and the prize?

Unparalleled Freedom and Peace

By shifting from a passive consumer to an active owner in all these areas – your thoughts, your beliefs, your actions – you empower yourself. You move from feeling like a victim of circumstance to becoming the proactive, badass agent in your own success and well-being. This kind of ownership fosters a deeper connection to your own process, sharpens your self-awareness, and ultimately strengthens that Marathon Mindset, enabling you to face any challenge with greater resilience and achieve your full, amazing potential.

Specifically, when you truly embrace ownership and release the grip of relentless consumerism, you will experience:

- **Unshakeable Confidence:** That nagging voice whispering "not enough"? It starts to fade from your script. You'll build a quiet, unwavering belief in your own inherent worth, because you're no longer seeking validation from external props or other people's reviews. Your self-worth becomes internally generated, and that, my friend, is bulletproof.

- **Laser-Sharp Clarity & Focus:** No more brain fog from information overload or decision fatigue from chasing every shiny plot twist. By intentionally filtering what you consume, your mind clears, your focus sharpens, and you gain the mental bandwidth to pursue what truly matters to you. Say hello to genuine productivity, not just endless retakes.

- **Profound Inner Peace & Less Anxiety:** You'll sever the chains of FOMO, FOPO, and FOWI (remember those?). When you're no longer constantly comparing, seeking approval, or catastrophizing, your nervous system can finally exhale. You'll experience a deep calm, an unburdened sense of serenity that the latest gadget or social media trend could never deliver.

- **Empowered Leadership in Your Own Story (and Beyond!):** This isn't just about directing others; it's about directing yourself. You'll become the visionary behind your own destiny, calling the shots, embracing responsibility for the narrative, and inspiring others by the sheer force of your authentic, self-directed life. You'll move from reacting to the script to writing and creating it.

This is your path to becoming the most vibrant, confident, and utterly free version of yourself. It's the ultimate upgrade, built not on accumulating more, but on radical self-ownership.

Your Permission Slip

This is it, folks. This is the moment you've been waiting for. It could be giving yourself that permission to finally go for that killer management position you've been eyeing. Or finally hitting "send" on that application for the graduate program that keeps calling your name. Maybe it's taking a calculated risk and fearlessly seeking out investors for that silent, but absolutely epic business idea you've been nurturing in your soul. Or perhaps, it's making the courageous, magnificent choice to step away from your job and embrace the profound journey of having a baby.

Whatever that deep, resonant desire is, know this: You are entitled to strive for what lights you up. This isn't a luxury; it's your birthright. It's your fundamental right as a human being, as a contributing member of society, as a global citizen. Stop waiting for a sign, for an external permission slip. The only approval you need is your own. This, my darling, is what taking ownership truly means.

What permission are you giving yourself today? How about permission to feel better? Permission to have nice things. Permission to feel safe.

The choice is yours.

7 Ways to Know You're an Owner, Not a Consumer

Alright, superstar, ready to find out if you're truly owning your life, or just letting it happen to you? This isn't about being perfect; it's about making conscious choices that scream, "I'm in charge here!"

7 WAYS TO BE AN OWNER
NOT A CONSUMER

1. You're the Vibe-Creator, Not the Scroll-Bot

You use social media as a tool to build, learn, or spread good vibes, not just to endlessly consume highlight reels that make you feel less-than.

2. You're the Head Chef of Your Own Plate

You consciously choose foods that genuinely nourish your body and fuel your brain. You own how you feel from the inside out, making your plate a source of power, not just convenience.

3. You Research & Digest News, Not Just Consume it

You actively seek diverse perspectives, question sources, and form your own informed opinions, rather than letting the 24/7 news cycle just wash over you. You own your understanding of the world.

4. You're the Director of Your Downtime Blockbuster

You curate entertainment with purpose, listening to audiobooks, watching podcasts that spark your soul, rather than letting an algorithm numb your brain with a random binge-watch.

5. Your Vacay is Epic and Fully Customized

You design adventures and getaways focused on rejuvenation, nature and peak experiences—not just chasing the cheapest last-minute deal or snapping selfies at hot destinations

6. Your Activity is Fueled by Fire, Not FOMO

You ditch the trendy fitness craze and engage in movement that truly invigorates your body and lights up your spirit. You find pure joy in the process of moving, because it fuels you.

7. You Are Actively Sculpting Your Future

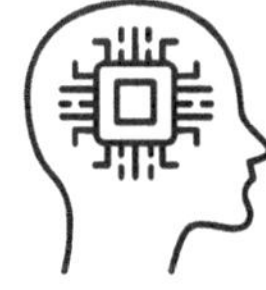

This is the big one: You know you're the primary force behind creating your happiness, health, and success. You take radical responsibility and build the life you crave, one intentional step at a time. You're the author, the architect, and the lead character of your unique, incredible story.

Ownership: Your Ultimate Finish Line

The crucial element of the entire Marathon Mindset, the one thing you absolutely must nail if you're going to truly conquer your course: it's about becoming an OWNER, not just a passive consumer.

This isn't just some feel-good mantra; it's your power move. It's time to take fierce ownership of your thoughts, your choices, and especially the information you allow to shape your world. Because when you do that something incredible happens.

You'll not only navigate those gnarly challenges – the serpents of your mind, blizzards of misinformation – but you'll also unlock a deeper, more profound understanding of yourself and your unique place in this wild, beautiful world. You'll find that inner voice, your own wise, unwavering guide, ready to lead you. And trust me, that guide won't just get you across the finish line; it'll propel you towards a more authentic, more purposeful, and utterly unstoppable life.

Own it. All of it.

Rules of the Road

- Here's the Finisher Medal for exploring the Digital Deluge that targets you.
- You learned about the brands that make the earth proud.
- You peeked into Inner and External Locus of Control
- You checked out ways to protect your head from Platforms and AI
- And you got to evaluate yourself in the Owner vs. Consumer checklist
- Ready for more juice in your engine?

Now, are you ready to hear how the original gangstas of running set the pace for the sport today? Get ready, because this is where legends are made, and the real history of owning the run begins.

Come with me to the next chapter.

CHAPTER 6

THE OG'S GUIDE TO RUNNING

You've just learned about the power of being an owner, not merely a consumer – taking fierce responsibility for your mindset, your choices, and your journey, rather than passively accepting what's handed to you. It's about tapping into your inner drive and shaping your own movie.

Now, let's take that concept and apply it to the very roots of running itself.

So you're a runner, right? You've got your fancy GPS watch, your breathable tech fabric, your perfectly formulated gels, and a playlist curated for peak performance. That's cute. But let me tell you, back in the day, running was a whole different beast. It was gritty, it was raw, and frankly, it was a little bit nuts.

Running is a primal part of human DNA. We have legs, we're born to move! Forget those blinky wristbands and bouncy carbon soles for a second. Let's rewind the clock, way back to when our ancestors were rocking loincloths and diving for cover from a thundering herd of woolly mammoths. How did they eat? How did they survive? Often, it was through something called **persistence hunting**. They weren't just consumers of their environment; they were owners of their survival, and their feet were their most vital tool. This is where the true OGs of running began.

Back When It Was Wild!

Imagine this: you're hungry. Really, really hungry. There's a gazelle out there in the distance, and while it's powerful and surprisingly fast in bursts, it's not built for endless runs. But here's the secret our ancestors figured out: that gazelle can't run forever. They'd work together, a human pack, trotting, jogging, and relentlessly following their prey, not trying to out-sprint it, but to simply outlast it.

They'd keep going, mile after grueling mile, under the relentless sun, until the animal literally collapsed from heat and exhaustion. This wasn't about raw speed; it was about unwavering persistence, about putting one foot in front of the other, hour after hour, until the job was done.

That's right, your great grandparents 10,000 times removed were basically ultra-marathoners, running for dinner! You carry that same unwavering persistence in your very bones.

Take that couch potato.

Fast forward a few millennia, and we meet Pheidippides, a professional long-distance runner. In 490 BC, Athens was facing a Persian invasion and desperately needed Spartan aid. He was dispatched and ran an astonishing 150 miles to Sparta in just two days to plead for help! He then ran another 150 grueling miles back to Athens to deliver Sparta's disappointing refusal.

While modern marathon legend has him running the short distance from Marathon to Athens, the historical truth is that Pheidippides was running epic, multi-day ultramarathon distances as a professional. The modern marathon race honors this primal, innate human capacity for long-distance effort—the same endurance your ancestors used to literally run for dinner. He was the original ultra-courier, a true champion of the ancient roads!

Running as a Spectator Sport: Welcome to the Coliseum!

But here's a fun twist: running wasn't always just about personal bests and solitary journeys. Believe it or not, for a period in history, it was a wildly popular spectator sport, drawing massive crowds to grand venues, much like boxing or horse racing today.

Enter the era of Pedestrianism in the late 19th century. This was competitive walking and running, often over incredible distances, and it became a national obsession, especially in America and Britain. Transport yourself: Thousands of screaming fans, packed into arenas like the original Madison Square Garden in New York City. We're talking standing-room-only, people climbing on chairs, breaking windows just to get a glimpse of the action!

These weren't your typical track meets. The most famous events were the "Six-Day Races," where athletes would literally walk and run laps around a small indoor track for six days straight, with only brief breaks for sleep or medical attention. The goal? To cover the most miles. The air would be thick with dust and tobacco smoke, brass bands would play, and the crowd would roar as their favorite "pedestrians" pushed themselves to the absolute brink. It was raw, grueling, and utterly captivating. Oh, and it was entertainment. It attracted celebrities, politicians, wealthy businessmen, public figures. Matter of fact, a future president to be – Teddy Roosevelt, who was a sportsman himself, attended these spectacles. And if you think FanDuel is new, think again. Betting, match fixing, bookmakers and odds were all part of the Pedestrianism circus.

Shea Stadium: Not Just for Baseball Anymore!

You know Shea Stadium. The site of the Beatles' legendary first concert in 1965. It also hosted a papal visit by Pope John Paul II in 1979. Oh, and let's not forget the "Miracle Mets" win the World Series in 1969, and again in 1986. Its distinctive "Home Run Apple" sculpture that has become part of franchise lore and instantly recognizable symbol of New York.

This is where Shea Stadium, the iconic home of the New York Mets, enters the ultrarunning narrative. The New York Road Runners Club (NYRRC), a driving force in the burgeoning running boom, began organizing 100-mile races in the late 1976. These events were often held on loops in Flushing Meadows-Corona Park. You know, the one with the Unisphere and the observation towers from the 1964 World's Fair?

But here's the mind-blowing part: sometimes, these 100 mile races were actually held right inside Shea Stadium itself, nowadays known as Citi Field. I mean, these weren't just some casual neighborhood jogs. The Athletics Congress, which was the big-deal predecessor to USA Track & Field even sanctioned them as the USA 100-mile Championship. How cool is that?!

Instead of baseball players hitting dingers and rounding the bases, you had these incredible ultrarunners. They were pushing their absolute limits for 100 miles, lap after exhausting lap, right there inside a major league stadium. It was this totally unique, almost surreal blend of a professional sports venue and the most extreme endurance test you could imagine.

And get this: Wayne actually ran a few of these 100 milers! His absolute favorite was the one at Shea Stadium. He'd start right at home plate, run past center field, head out into the parking lot, then return to the stadium at 3rd base, and finish the mile loop back at home plate. He likes to say he's crossed home plate more times than most professional baseball players do in a season.

Wait, Jogging is Good for You?

Now, let's fast forward a bit, because this is what it was like in the good old days, before running was even considered "exercise" by most sane people. In fact, the word "jog" didn't even exist in the fitness lexicon until the legendary Arthur Lydiard came along in the mid 1950s. This New Zealand coach, bless his revolutionary heart, basically told the world, "Hey, this running thing? It's actually good for you!"

And Lydiard wasn't just about turning average Joes into marathoners. He was a significant pioneer in cardiac rehabilitation. In the early 1960s, Lydiard was asked to train a group of heart patients in Auckland, New Zealand using easy distance running. This was revolutionary at the time, because the standard medical advice for heart attack recovery back then was... wait for it... prolonged bed rest. Lydiard proved that running, even gentle jogging, could be a powerful tool for rehabilitation and overall heart health, long before it was mainstream.

And thus, the modern running movement was born. It became a path to health, happiness, and maybe a little bit of glorious suffering.

Running Shoes and a Family Feud

Sneakers, trainers, kicks, gym shoes, plimsolls, tennis shoes, track shoes, cross-trainers... whatever you call them, they all serve the same purpose: to help you move! But have you ever stopped to think where your trusty running shoes really came from? Did you know that for the longest time, what passed for running shoes were often just flimsy material sewn onto thin, unsupportive rubber soles? Not exactly high-performance, right? You basically ran in slightly glorified slippers!

And for the longest time, the shoe market was dominated by two titans, born from an incredible family drama: Adidas and Puma. These weren't just rival companies; they were founded by brothers who had a legendary falling out. Adi Dassler founded Adidas, and his brother, Rudolf Dassler, went on to create Puma. Their footwear was already making waves in international competitions as early as the late 1920s, with athletes sporting their innovative spiked shoes. This sibling rivalry was so intense, it literally divided their hometown in Germany, with people choosing sides based on the shoes they wore! So, for decades, if you were an athlete, you were likely wearing a Dassler brother's creation.

A Determined Coach and a Breakfast Appliance

But even with the German giants dominating, the shoes themselves still had a long way to go. And at the heart of transforming this footwear wasteland was Bill Bowerman, the legendary track coach of Steve Prefontaine at the University of Oregon.

Now, Bill wasn't just any coach; he was utterly, completely obsessed. Obsessed with making his athletes faster, better, stronger. And he quickly realized that the clunky, heavy, ill-fitting running shoes of the era were holding them back. He literally took existing shoes apart with a band saw in his garage, meticulously trying to figure out how to shave off ounces, improve traction, and add just the right amount of support. He was a tinkerer, a mad scientist of footwear, driven by one simple, relentless question: *How can I make a better shoe?*

This obsession led to one of the most iconic "aha!" moments in sports history: the waffle iron. The story goes that in 1971, while having breakfast with his wife, Barbara, Bill looked at her waffle iron. He saw the grid pattern, the raised nubs, and a lightbulb went off in his head. What if a sole could have that kind of pattern? It would provide amazing traction without needing heavy metal spikes, and it would be lightweight. So, in a moment of pure, unadulterated genius (and probably a ruined kitchen appliance), he poured liquid rubber into the waffle iron. The result? A prototype for a revolutionary new sole design that would provide unprecedented grip on various surfaces. That's right, your cutting-edge running shoes probably have a distant, delicious relative in a breakfast appliance!

Now, enter Phil Knight, one of Bowerman's former runners. Phil was a bit of a dreamer, fresh out of business school, and he had a "crazy idea" (as he calls it in the iconic book Shoe Dog). He'd written a paper arguing that Japanese-made running shoes, with their high quality and lower cost, could disrupt the German-dominated athletic shoe market in the U.S. So, in 1964, with a $50 loan from his dad, he started Blue Ribbon Sports (BRS), initially importing and selling Onitsuka Tiger shoes out of the trunk of his car at track meets.

He sent some samples to Bowerman, hoping for an order. Instead, he got a business partner! Bowerman was impressed and joined forces, bringing his relentless drive for innovation to the nascent company. While Knight handled the business side, the sales, and the constant struggle for cash flow, Bowerman was the product visionary, always experimenting, always pushing the boundaries of shoe design.

The "waffle sole" concept, patented in 1974, became the cornerstone of their first truly groundbreaking shoe, the Nike Waffle Trainer. This shoe was a game-changer, offering lightweight comfort and superior traction that runners had never experienced. The success of the Waffle Trainer, combined with their eventual split from Onitsuka created the need for their own brand.

From Waffle Iron to Global Empire

As BRS grew they desperately needed a new name for their brand. Phil Knight, the co-founder, had his own suggestion: "Dimension Six", which was rejected by everyone.

The clock was ticking, with a factory deadline looming. In a moment of pure inspiration, or perhaps desperation, Jeff Johnson, one of the company's first employees, came up with the name. He claimed it came to him in a dream: Nike.

"What's a Nike?" Phil Knight reportedly asked.

Johnson's reply was simple: "The Greek Goddess of Victory."

And just like that, a legend was born in 1971. Nike was the winged Greek goddess personifying triumph, speed and strength, often depicted soaring through the skies to deliver success in both military battles and athletic competitions. She symbolized ultimate achievement.

The name was short, memorable and had a powerful "K" sound that resonated. While Phil Knight initially wasn't thrilled ("Well, I don't love it, but maybe it will grow on me," he famously said), the name stuck. It perfectly encapsulated the brand's aspirations: to empower athletes to achieve victory, to push limits, and to embody the spirit of triumph. The iconic "Swoosh" logo, designed by Carolyn Davidson for a mere $35, is even said to represent the wing of the goddess Nike, further cementing this powerful connection to victory and motion.

All thanks to a coach who just wanted his runners to be a little bit faster, and a waffle iron.

Old School Gear & Glorious Lack of Tech

You know how now you've got all your sleek, aerodynamic, perfectly-fitted gear? Forget all that. Back in the day, "performance wear" meant something entirely different. In fact, if we're talking about the *original* runners – those in the ancient Olympic Games – "performance wear" meant **nothing at all**. That's right, the ancient Greeks competed naked. This wasn't just for shock value; it was believed to offer maximum freedom of movement, celebrate the beauty of the human form, and serve as a tribute to the gods. So, when you picture the first marathoners, imagine them entirely unencumbered by fabric!

Fast forward a few millennia to the early days of modern distance running, and while clothes were definitely back in fashion, it was still less about "tech" and more about "let's hope this doesn't chafe too badly or I don't freeze to death."

For winter wonderland wear, your high-tech layering system was basically... thermal underwear. You don't know what that is? Go ask your Grandpa! No sleek, breathable, moisture-wicking Vuori outfits here! You literally bundled up like the Michelin Man, often in scratchy wool or thick cotton long johns, and just prayed for the best. Sweating was a given, and staying dry? That was a distant, glorious dream. You'd finish a winter run looking like you'd wrestled a yeti and lost, but hey, you were warm.

And fashion statements? Forget the haute couture of today; back then, "singlets" were the uniform. These bad boys were crafted from polyester or some other space-age synthetic blend, all engineered for one glorious purpose: to wick sweat away from your skin, fast. And did they? Mostly! You'd still finish a race looking like you'd taken a dip in a swamp, but at least your top wasn't clinging to you like a soggy second skin.

These athletic wonders typically sported a snug, no-flapping-allowed fit (because, trust me, chafing is the arch-nemesis of any long-distance runner). They often came with a "racerback" design or those narrower shoulder straps, giving your arms and shoulders maximum freedom to pump, pump, pump. And for a splash of flair? These weren't just plain white tees. Singlets were where team colors truly shone! Take legendary runner Steve Prefontaine, for instance. He rocked a "glossy-purple" singlet in high school and later donned the "ethereal Oregon singlet" – a vibrant green and yellow that practically screamed speed. It was less about runway fashion and more about showing your colors and getting the job done, sweat and all.

Herstory on the Run: The Unstoppable Momentum

The pioneers we've celebrated fought themselves and the terrain, but the women who followed faced an even fiercer opponent: institutional resistance. For generations, women were actively banned from running long distances, deemed too fragile for the marathon. The true act of endurance for these trailblazers was claiming the right to compete at all.

This initial defiance came in two powerful waves. 1966 when denied entry to the Boston Marathon, Bobbi Gibb literally hid in the bushes near the start line and jumped into the race after the gun sounded, completing the entire course unofficially. She proved the physical feat was achievable, running "bandit" to show that the female body was undeniably built for endurance.

A year after Gibb proved it was possible, Kathrine Switzer forced the institutional reckoning. By registering as "K.V. Switzer," she received the historic bib Number 261, compelling the organizers to recognize her presence. Her moment was pure defiance: when the race official attempted to tear her number off her chest, the iconic photograph of the struggle became the watershed image that finally signaled the end of the exclusion era. The marathon was officially opened to women in 1972.

The Silent Revolution: Unleashing the Power of the Sports Bra

But even as these trailblazers were out there shattering records and proving everyone wrong, they hit another major snag: gear designed almost exclusively for men. Can you even imagine trying to conquer a marathon in saggy men's shorts and a regular old bra that offered, like, zero, zilch, nada support? Your girls would be doing their own separate marathon!

That sheer, unadulterated frustration gave birth to a truly brilliant, Original Gangster innovation. Avid runner Lisa Lindahl was tired of the traditional bra failing her mid-stride. So, she teamed up with her friend, costume designer Polly Smith, for an inspired—and totally bizarre— solution. Check this out: The resourceful duo took two men's jockstraps and famously sewed them together. And voila! The sports bra was born. That's right—your trusty, bounce-busting, life-changing support garment? It's got jockstrap DNA.

Nipple Rot

Seriously now, look away if the sight of blood makes you queasy. Because this was, and honestly, still is, the silent dirge of many runners. The constant chafing and rubbing of that fabric across sweaty nipples, mile after mile, causes the dreaded "nipple rot". Any marathoner, especially a guy, will tell you. You'd finish a race, peel off that singlet, and there it would be: a tell-tale streak of red. "Yup," they'd wince, "man are my nipples are raw!" It was a painful badge of honor, a testament to the fact that sometimes, even the most high-tech gear couldn't solve every problem. A little bit of Vaseline became every male runner's best friend.

Comfort and style were so secondary to just, you know, running. Nobody was thinking about Instagram-worthy outfits or matching their socks to their shoes. The goal was purely functional: cover your body, and don't get arrested!

Running on Empty, and Sugar

Let's talk about fueling the machine, because this is where things get truly hilarious. Gels? Energy chews? Fancy electrolyte drinks with specific ratios and milligrams? Pfft! You guys, we were living in the Stone Age of sports nutrition!

Back then, "sports drink" meant one thing: Coke! It was the high-performance fuel of choice. That's right, a sugary, bubbly burst of pure caffeine and simple carbs. You'd be out there, miles into a run, and then you'd hit a water stop. You'd grab a paper cup of warm, flat Coca-Cola, chug it down, feel that immediate, slightly nauseating sugar rush, and then probably burp your way through the next mile. It was a glorious, chaotic, and utterly unscientific approach. They weren't worried about glycogen stores or muscle recovery; they were just trying to keep the lights on!

And hydration? Oh, my sweet jogger, hydration was often an afterthought. They weren't meticulously tracking fluid intake, carrying fancy backpack bladders, or even thinking about sodium levels. If there was a water fountain, great. If not? Well, you just got thirstier.

Which brings me to "bonking." For those of you who've never experienced it, "bonking" isn't just getting tired. It's like your body suddenly decides, "Nope! We're done here!" It's a sudden, dramatic, full-system shutdown. Your legs turn to lead, your brain fogs over, and you literally feel like you're running through quicksand. And back then, it wasn't something to be avoided, it was a rite of passage! If you hadn't bonked at least once, were you even really trying? It was a badge of honor, a testament to your sheer determination to push past the point of no return. Stumble across the finish line, wrecked but with a perverse sense of pride that they had pushed their bodies to that absolute limit.

Fueled by little more than sugar water and pure stubbornness.

The OG Eyeroll

So how do the old timer runners view the hyper-engineered sports nutrition products now?

First off, there's definitely a chuckle when they see someone meticulously planning out their gel intake every 30 minutes, or debating the merits of chews over power bars. They're like, "Back in my day, we had flat Coke and a prayer! And maybe an orange slice if we were lucky!" To many, the idea of something specifically designed to be consumed while running, in a gooey packet, still feels a bit... alien.

Many old-school runners relied on more "real" food – bananas, pretzels, even baked potatoes. These were the pioneers of performance foods. There's a sentiment that if you trained hard enough, your body should be able to handle it with more traditional fuel. The thought of all those processed sugars and chemicals can sometimes raise an eyebrow.

However, even the most traditional "old timers" can't deny the science. They know why those simple carbs and electrolytes are so important, and why bonking happened so often. Modern sports nutrition products are engineered for quick absorption and to minimize stomach issues, which is a huge step up from a gut full of fizzy soda! They're convenient, easy to carry, and they absolutely help prevent that dreaded "wall" from hitting you quite so hard.

So, while they might joke about their "fuel for the futile" days, and maybe still prefer a banana over a gel for a long run, most veteran runners acknowledge that these new products have made endurance running more accessible and, frankly, less painful. It's just that for them, the grit of pushing through without all the bells and whistles was part of the charm, and the suffering!

RunMan

You know how you just pop in your tiny earbuds, hit play on your phone, and you've got a million songs at your fingertips? Yeah, that was pure science fiction for the OGs!

Before the late 70s, if you were running, you were either listening to the sounds of nature or traffic. Or maybe you had a running buddy and you just... talked. Imagine that! The idea of a personal soundtrack for your run simply didn't exist in a portable way.

Then came the transistor radios in the 60s and 70s. These were small, but still pretty clunky, usually with a tiny, tinny speaker. If you wanted to listen, you'd have to hold it up to your ear, or maybe try to balance it on your shoulder. Running with one? Forget about it! It was like trying to run with a brick glued to your head. And you were stuck listening to whatever the radio station was playing – no personal playlists there!

But then, in 1979, everything changed. Enter the Sony Walkman. Oh. My. God. This was the game-changer! Suddenly, you could actually carry your own music with you. It was a portable cassette player, and while it was still a "brick" by today's standards, it was revolutionary.

The Headphone Hustle

The headphones that came with the early Walkman were also a far cry from your sleek AirPods. They were these lightweight (for the time, anyway!) on-ear headphones. Not tiny earbuds that disappear, but actual headphones that perched on your ears, connected by a band over your head.

So, you'd have this Walkman, maybe tucked into a fanny pack (yes, those were a thing, and yes, we wore them!), or if you were really brave, you'd try to rig it to your waistband or even, as I mentioned before, strap it to your chest. Then you'd have these wires, constantly tangling, flapping, and threatening to yank the headphones off your head with every stride.

And the sound quality? It was stereo, which was amazing for the time, but it wasn't exactly noise-canceling. You could still hear the world around you, which was probably a good thing for safety, but it wasn't the immersive experience we get now. Some early Walkmans even had a "Hot Line" button that would mute the music and turn on a built-in microphone so you could talk to someone without taking off your headphones.

It's funny how things come full circle, isn't it? We went from those big, clunky early headphones, then shrunk down to the almost invisible earbuds of today. But now, the pendulum is swinging back. Walk through any city, and you'll see a new generation embracing oversized, retro-style headphones – the kind that look like giant ear muffs, or "Princess Leia buns". They're back, not for lack of choice, but as a deliberate fashion statement, a nostalgic nod to the very "Headphone Hustle" the OGs endured.

The Legends

You know, we've talked about the gear, the fuel, and even the wild places to run. But then there are the true OGs, the ones who didn't just run; they absolutely conquered. These were the pioneers of extreme endurance, pushing human limits so far they practically redefined what was possible. They didn't just participate; they owned challenges that seemed utterly impossible to the rest of us.

You know a standard marathon is a grueling 26.2 miles, right? Well, an ultramarathon takes that distance and laughs in its face. We're talking:

- 50 kilometers (that's about 31 miles): Often considered the entry-level ultra, a great stepping stone for marathoners.

- 50 miles: This often takes 8-14 hours or more to complete, depending on the terrain and the runner.

- 100 kilometers (about 62 miles): A common distance for those aiming for 100-mile races later.

- 100 miles: The gold standard or holy grail for many ultra-runners, pushing mental and physical limits. Think iconic races like the brutal Western States 100 or the high-altitude Leadville 100, where runners push through a staggering 100 miles of relentless terrain.

- And then the truly bonkers 200 miles or more: These are extreme challenges, pushing mental and physical limits, with examples like the Moab 240 or Tahoe 200.

But it gets even wilder! Ultras also include timed races. Instead of a set distance, you run for a predetermined amount of time, and the goal is to cover as much ground as humanly possible before the clock runs out. Imagine running for 24 hours straight, or 48 hours, or even multi-day events where sleep is a luxury you can barely afford!

While countless ultrarunners deserve recognition, I'm spotlighting a few whose monumental achievements didn't just break records, but fundamentally reshaped running, and in some cases, society itself.

Marshall Ulrich: The Endurance King

This guy, Marshall Ulrich, is a living, breathing legend. Seriously, if you look up "endurance" in the dictionary, his picture should be there. He didn't just finish, but dominated, over 125 ultramarathons!

Now Marshall's signature feat? The brutal Badwater Ultramarathon, a 135-mile race across Death Valley, in **July**. Imagine that heat! And he's done it multiple times, often self-supported, carrying all his own gear. That's not just running; that's an act of defiance against nature itself.

But he didn't stop there. he also climbed the Seven Summits – you know, the highest peaks on every continent, including Mount Everest! And, get this, he once ran 3,063.2 miles from San Francisco to New York in just 52.5 days! That's like running two marathons a day, every single day, for almost two months. My mind just short-circuits trying to comprehend that.

Marshall perfectly embodies ownership because he consistently seeks the absolute edge of human capability. He lives by his own mantra: "Find out what you're made of: it's more than you think."

I had the privilege of asking Marshall how he stays in a positive mindset. He replied:

> "I try not to overthink or complicate things (mindf*$! myself to be blunt), just get out, get started and do it. When things get tough, I remind myself that I am the one that is responsible for getting myself into whatever it is I'm doing (so I have no one to blame but myself). That's kinda like a slap in the face and wakes me up."

And when I ask what keeps him motivated, he replied:

> "It's a commitment to myself and others to be the best I can. And most of all I DO NOT consider myself the crème de la crème of runners. I always say that: "I know I'm in trouble when I take myself too seriously."

And what's the Endurance King up to now? Marshall's still conquering, but in new ways! He's inspiring readers as an author, wowing crowds as a speaker on cruise ships. And with his wife Heather, he's the powerhouse race director of the Route 66 UltraRun.

Joan Benoit Samuelson: The Pioneer of Possibility

If Marshall Ulrich redefined the duration of human endurance, Joan Benoit Samuelson redefined its possibility for an entire gender. She is, quite simply, the OG of modern women's distance running. Her feats weren't just about speed; they were about claiming space in history where none existed before.

Her signature conquest? The 1984 Los Angeles Olympic Games, which hosted the first-ever Women's Olympic Marathon. This wasn't just a race; it was a political and cultural statement that generations of female athletes had fought for. In a moment of intense global scrutiny, Joan didn't wait— she took radical ownership of the narrative.

She famously broke away from the pack just three miles into the race, executing an act of audacity that stunned commentators and competitors alike. She held that lead to win the gold medal, not only solidifying her place as the first women's champion but proving that sustained, high-level female endurance belonged on the world stage. She had already proven her mettle by shattering the World Record at the 1983 Boston Marathon with a time of 2:22:43—a time that was incomprehensibly fast for the era.

But the ultimate expression of her ownership came just 17 days before the Olympic Trials when she underwent emergency knee surgery. Instead of surrendering to pain and prognosis, she harnessed the Crisis Mentality, taking total command of her physical reality and showing up at the start line. Her message, like Marshall's, is clear: limits are merely suggestions until you decide to own the outcome. She literally ran straight through a medical crisis to claim her destiny.

Mark Burnett: From Eco-Challenge to Reality TV Empire

Now, let's talk about another kind of ownership, one that changed our living rooms forever. Before he became the mastermind behind Survivor, Mark Burnett was deep in the world of extreme endurance. He didn't just produce these shows; he actually competed in the Raid Gauloises, an expedition-length adventure race. This wasn't your typical marathon; it was a multi-day, multi-sport, non-stop race through brutal, untamed wilderness, pushing teams to their absolute breaking point, physically and mentally.

That experience sparked something in him. Burnett realized the raw, unscripted drama of human endurance and competition, the real struggles, triumphs, and failures he witnessed in these extreme races, had incredible television potential. This led him to create the Eco-Challenge: The Expedition Race. Imagine watching teams navigate treacherous terrain, battle sleep deprivation, and push their bodies beyond anything you thought possible – all in real-time.

Of course, these exact brutal conditions don't exist in the "actual world" for most people, so Burnett, with a stroke of genius (and maybe a touch of prophetic vision), took that "fly by the seat of your pants" expedition race concept and altered the script. He made it more challenging, yes, but also more scripted, and, let's be honest, more UN-real for mass consumption. He took the essence of extreme endurance and packaged it for television.

Race Day Rewards and Culinary Curiosities

Alright, let's talk about the payoff, the grand finale, the moment you crossed that finish line back in the day. Because race day rewards and post-race feasts? They were a whole different beast. Forget your sleek, participation trophies and artisanal food trucks. This was about practicality, pure grit, and sometimes, hilariously random keepsakes.

The Swag Bag: Bottle Openers, Sporks, and the Holy Grail Buckle

Old time runners could look forward to minimal swag on race day, generally a t-shirt at a small race. The bigger the race, the better the swag, the standard t-shirt, and maybe a hat, or a pair of shorts.

Today, you get tech gadgets, fancy protein bars, and t-shirts made of space-age fabric. Back then, your "swag bag" was less about marketing and more about stuff you might actually use. You might get a bottle opener – because after running for hours, priorities, right?! You needed to crack open that post-race beverage! Or maybe a spork – the ultimate multi-purpose utensil for all your camping and questionable post-race culinary needs.

And if you were truly lucky, especially at one of those insane ultras, the real prize wasn't a medal to hang on a wall. It was a solid, heavy, beautifully crafted buckle for your belt. That buckle wasn't just a piece of metal; it was a badge of honor, a tangible testament to the sheer, unadulterated suffering and triumph you'd just endured. Medals and t-shirts were the standard, sure, but the truly unique items were the ones that made you scratch your head, smile, and think, "Only this race would give me that." Race swag wasn't about participation trophies; it was about practical (and sometimes hilariously random) keepsakes.

Post-Race Feasts: Hearty, Local, and Gloriously Unfussy

Okay, you guys, let's dive even deeper into the glorious, sometimes baffling, world of post-race culinary curiosities from back in the day! Because while modern races have their standardized, scientifically formulated recovery zones, the old-school finish lines were a truly unique feast for the senses, and your depleted stomach. Forget your quinoa bowls and gluten-free pastries. This was about fueling a body that had just been through a war.

Western States 100: Bacon, Quesadillas, and a Full-Blown Buffet

Now, if you want to talk about real food at an aid station, the Western States 100-Mile Endurance Run has always been famous for it. This race is a beast, going from Squaw Valley to Auburn, California, over mountains and through canyons. By the time you hit some of those later aid stations, your stomach is probably rebelling against anything sweet.

So what do they offer? It's not just gels and chews. You might find bacon! Yes, crispy, salty bacon. Or little quesadillas, maybe some mashed potatoes, or even ramen noodles. I've heard stories of runners absolutely craving savory, salty, real food, and these aid stations delivered. It's like a mini-diner in the middle of nowhere, and it's exactly what your body, tired of all the sugar, starts to scream for.

The Comrades Marathon: Soup, Potatoes, and Pure Comfort

Let's check out the Comrades Marathon in South Africa. This isn't just any marathon; it's an ultra-marathon, one of the oldest and most legendary in the world, running nearly 90 kilometers (56 miles!) between two cities. After that kind of effort, your body isn't asking for a tiny protein bite; it's begging for sustenance.

And what did they give you? Beyond the usual water and flat Coke, you'd find aid stations and the finish line offering things like boiled potatoes, often with salt. Simple, right? But after hours of sweating, that salty carb hit is pure gold! And as you got into the later stages, especially at night, they have hot soup. Imagine running for 10, 12, 15 hours, and suddenly, a warm, salty broth hits your system. It's not just food; it's a mental reset, a hug for your insides. It was about practical, easily digestible, comforting fuel that spoke to the soul of a truly exhausted runner.

The Boston Marathon: Beyond the Beef Stew

The Boston Marathon is traditionally held on Patriots' Day, which is the third Monday in April. This holiday commemorates the battles of Lexington and Concord, marking the start of the American Revolutionary War. What do they serve at this famous race? Beef stew. Think about the general vibe: hearty, traditional New England fare. You aren't getting fancy smoothies; you were getting solid, recognizable food. Maybe some simple bread, fruit, and whatever local, no-frills sustenance could be quickly distributed to thousands of exhausted runners. It was about the shared experience of having conquered that historic course, and the food was just a part of that no-nonsense, hard-earned reward.

My personal favorite race food? Maui Chips. Best Chips on Earth. After conquering a brutal course in Kauai, Kona, Maui or Honolulu I look for the simple, glorious aluminum trays of these chips. Salty, crunchy, and exactly what your depleted body craves. It isn't gourmet. It is hearty, local, and real.

Rule #5

If you've ever dipped a toe into the serious (and sometimes seriously intense) world of road cycling, you might have stumbled upon the Velominati Rules. These aren't official UCI regulations, but rather a tongue-in-cheek, yet fiercely adhered-to, set of commandments for the discerning cyclist. They originated from the Velominati website, founded by Frank Strack and

Brett Kennedy, as a way to celebrate the history, traditions, and aesthetics of road cycling with a distinctive blend of irreverence and humor.

Think of them as a "code of conduct" for those who truly love the sport, covering everything from proper gear etiquette to mental fortitude. They're designed to inspire, amuse, and sometimes, gently, or not so gently, mock those who deviate from the "proper" way of cycling.

Some famous Rules include:

- The bikes on top of your car should be worth more than the car. A playful jab at priorities in a cyclist's life.
- If you are out riding in bad weather, it means you are a badass. Celebrating grit and dedication over fair-weather riding.

And my absolute favorite rule: Rule #5: Harden the Fuck Up. Perhaps the most famous and often quoted. It's about pushing through discomfort, pain, and not complaining.

Now, here's a wild idea, and it might get me in trouble, but let's be honest. There's a strong perception that younger generations are a little averse to hard work and toughening up. They've been raised in a different world, one that rightly prioritizes mental health and setting boundaries. So a mantra like Rule #5 can sound less like a challenge and more like a cruel joke.

But here's the thing: we've got to find the middle ground. The Marathon Mindset isn't about mindless suffering or pushing yourself to the point of burnout. It's about knowing the difference between healthy discomfort that leads to growth. You have to learn when to listen to your body, and when to tell your inner voice of doubt to shut the hell up. Rule #5 is a tool for that exact moment—it's not a lifestyle, it's a strategy for the last mile.

The Power of Postponement

The reason we struggle with Rule #5 is that it requires a fundamental skill that has become increasingly rare in our instant-delivery world: delayed gratification.

Delayed gratification is the ability to resist the temptation for an immediate reward in favor of a later, more substantial reward. It is the core mechanism that allows us to bypass the short-term comfort (quitting the run, hitting snooze, spending the money) for the long-term achievement (the finish line, the career growth, the financial freedom).

Not Everybody Gets a Trophy

And this, my friends, brings me to a fundamental truth that might ruffle a few feathers in our modern, participation-trophy-obsessed world: not everybody gets a trophy.

Guess what? It takes work to reach your goals. Real, tenacious, sweat-equity. The true measure of your passion isn't just how much you want something; it's how much you're willing to endure to get it. This isn't about being exclusionary; it's about reinforcing an inevitable, powerful truth: your passion is worth fighting for.

Giving a trophy to everybody, simply for showing up, diminishes the hard-won accomplishments of those who truly invest, sacrifice, and achieve. It dilutes the very meaning of effort. And this rule, born on the unforgiving trails and relentless roads of endurance sports, applies far beyond the finish line.

Performance Paradox

Look at it from a leadership paradigm. You have a handful of high-performing employees who consistently go above and beyond. Then you have the majority in the middle, doing solid work. And, let's be honest, a few lagging far behind in performance and drive. Giving everyone the same recognition, the same "trophy," or an equal bonus does two profoundly damaging things:

1. It incentivizes laggard performance. Why push harder if the reward is the same for minimal effort?

2. It demotivates the high performers. When their exceptional dedication isn't acknowledged and rewarded proportionally, their commitment wanes. They see their extra effort treated as equal to someone else's minimal output, and the fire begins to dim.

This isn't about creating an unfair system; it's about recognizing that there's a crucial difference between a "high performer" (someone who does their job well) and a "high achiever" (someone who consistently exceeds expectations, sets new benchmarks, and drives innovation). This distinction isn't just about performance, it's about impact.

Managers who adopt a flat organizational model, treating everyone the same regardless of achievements, goal attainment, objectives, or performance, unwittingly sabotage their best talent. Do you know what this does? It crushes the spirit of those who are truly committed. It actively destroys the entrepreneurial drive of people who are inherently driven, who envision a higher purpose, and who strive for a more elevated life.

So, whether you're rocking the latest tech or channeling your inner OG, the core of the Marathon Mindset remains the same. It's about showing up, putting in the work, and owning every glorious, messy, triumphant step of your unique journey. It's about knowing that the greatest rewards aren't handed out; they're earned through sweat, perseverance, and the unwavering belief in yourself.

Rules of the Road

Just for sticking with me through this wild ride, you've earned some serious cred!

- You get a Finisher Medal for learning about the OGs of running.

- Who knew your ancestors were ultra runners?

- You explored the fascinating, sometimes hilarious, evolution of running shoes. Waffles, anyone?

- You delved into the sometimes questionable, but effective, fashion and fueling strategies that powered these early legends. Flat Coke, baby!

- You got the inside scoop on how sports bras were engineered. Jockstrap DNA.

And you even got an inside look at why everybody does NOT get a trophy, and how that applies to the racecourse as well as the corporate boardroom. Because purpose earns its own rewards!

So with all that sweat and wisdom under your belt, are you ready to hear the one big **recovery secret** that runners, especially the OGs, have always known? Turn the page.

CHAPTER 7

NATURE THE RESTORER

Ever found yourself at a dinner meeting, maybe mid-chew at a swanky spot, when someone shoots you that look—the one that clearly says, "Put that phone away!"?

We've all been there, haven't we? Maybe it's not a dinner, but you're in a regular meeting, pretending to take notes, but your thumbs are flying across the screen. What's so urgent, so captivating that it pulls your attention away from the actual humans in the room? It could be the stock market ticker giving you a tiny jolt, or perhaps the siren song of your favorite TikToker posting vacation reels with her adorable Corgi. Maybe it's even just an email from work—because the work never truly stops, does it? That little screen becomes a portal to another world, one that feels more demanding, more immediate, than the one right in front of you.

And then, as you reluctantly tap the screen off and slide it into your pocket, do you feel that tiny, irrational pang of panic? Like you're suddenly disconnected from the very lifeline of the universe? It's a real thing, that little jolt of separation anxiety from our digital companions.

My husband gave me an Apple Watch for my birthday last year. He offered to set it up for me, and the conversation went something like this:

Wayne: Do you want to get email notifications?

Rekha: Nope.

Wayne: How about text notifications?

Rekha: Nah.

Wayne: Okay, so what alerts do you want?

Rekha: None.

Wayne: Then what exactly do you want it for?

Rekha: I just want to track my steps and calorie burn.

I'm an accomplished insomniac. Why do I need a watch to tell me I suck at sleeping?

Because that gadget isn't just measuring your sleep; it's holding a mirror up to your mind. All that 2:30 AM restlessness, that churning anxiety you can't quite shake? It's a symptom. And the root of the problem is so primitive, it's grim.

Why Your Brain Thinks Your To-Do List is a Tiger

In Chapter 2, you read why we're pretty much wired for negativity. It was a handy little trait that kept us alive back in the day. But now, let's yank the curtain back on what's really going on here.

That ancient brain of ours, constantly on the lookout for a lion in the grass, has been completely hijacked by the modern world. Our brains can't tell the difference between a charging bear and an email from an angry client. We get that same rush of adrenaline and cortisol, but we just sit there in our chair, and the stress has **nowhere to go**.

This primitive behavior has led us down a slippery slope:

Distraction leads to loss of focus.

Loss of focus leads to lame performance at work and school.

Lame performance leads to anxiety.

And anxiety, my friend, is a one-way ticket to stress.

You've heard the warnings: Stress is the ultimate killer. And you? You wave it off with a casual shrug, "Whatever. That's for the weak ones, the ones who actually unravel. Me? I'm a fortress. I'm absolutely fine." Are you? If you're like 40% of the planet, you're impacted by stress.

And the wild part? Our brains are still running on millennial-aged software. And that software doesn't have an optional *Calm The Nerves* setting. Evolution did a fantastic job of creating a fight or flight response for survival, but our primordial brains never evolved a mechanism to deal with the constant, modern stress.

So, on top of all the everyday stuff, we have to contend with the Algorithm of Outrage. Yes, it's a real thing, and it's a serious problem. Social media and the news are literally designed to keep us on high alert. They feed us content that makes us angry, scared, or outraged because, let's be honest, that stuff keeps us glued to the screen. It's a deliberate design to trigger our ancient survival response.

| Because a Panicked Brain is an Addicted Brain

And here's the kicker: that outrage extends way beyond your phone. All that fury built up from a steady diet of fabricated posts and fear-mongering news doesn't just stay online. It creeps into real life, venting itself out in your car, at the grocery store, or even at home.

Don't believe me? Think about your drive this morning.

The Wild West of the Road

I swear, every time I get behind the wheel these days, I feel like I've accidentally driven onto a movie set for Mad Max! Seriously, have you hopped behind the wheel lately? There are no rules, no logic, just a free-for-all where everyone does exactly what they want, whether it's legal or not. People are zipping through lanes like they're playing Grand Theft Auto, cutting others off without a second thought, and oh yes, cruising along with **headphones** on, completely oblivious to their surroundings and everyone else. Yo! can you hear that car beeping behind you? Can you hear the ambulance sirens down the road?

Being stuck in a traffic jam is a classic example of this madness. You're physically trapped, you have no control, and you're racing against the clock. Your body feels that frustration and helplessness as a threat, and it pumps you full of stress hormones. All you can do is sit there and fume, which just keeps the stress churning like a dishwasher on the power boost cycle.

It's such a stark contrast to how I learned to drive. I remember my Driver's Ed instructor Mr. Nicky, bless his militant soul, drilling defensive driving into us. It was this whole cautious concept of anticipating what might happen next, scanning the road like a hawk, and adjusting your actions to protect yourself and others. It was about courtesy, about shared responsibility, about, you know, not being a menace! Now, it feels like that entire concept has completely vanished basic courtesy and situational awareness, perfectly mirrors that larger societal trend of individualism run amok. It's as if the moment people slide into the driver's seat, they instantly lose all sense of collective accountability. And because they're straddling 5000 pounds of metal–Poof! Gone!

Always On. Always Exhausted.

And then there's the incessant need to be plugged into someone else. Why?

Have you ever noticed how allergic we are to silence? You see people on Bluetooth while hunting for deals at TJ Maxx, having an intense Zoom meeting while waiting for coffee, or even mid-treadmill run, glued to their phone. We are constantly feeding the void, afraid of a single, quiet moment.

I was riding the commuter train back from Penn Station, New York, trying to soak up the skyline—because a girl needs views, you know? A young Gen Zer sat down next to me, flashed the conductor his digital ticket, and resumed a conversation on speakerphone. Not only was it loud, but he proceeded to air every cringey detail of his date the night before: from the $28 cocktail she dared to order, to her skintight dress, to the exact reasons he was already composing a ghosting text. It was such a grotesque overshare, I felt like I needed to check him for a HIPAA violation.

Why do we do this? We overshare, over-connect, and over-schedule until we're depleted. It's almost like we're terrified of being alone with the most challenging person we know: Ourselves. We gorge on constant noise, but the price we pay is mental exhaustion and the complete lack of focus.

From Noise Addiction to Theta Zone

That chaotic, public performance on the train—that's just one symptom of the modern mind's addiction to noise. We're constantly doomscrolling, listening, talking, and filling every silent space. We're running, but we're running away from ourselves and straight into mental exhaustion.

But what if I told you the opposite of that frazzled, over-connected state is hidden in the simple rhythm of putting one foot in front of the other? When you run, after the first few miles of resistance, your brain shifts gears. You move out of that frantic, surface-level thinking and drop into the Theta Brain Wave State. That's the deep, meditative, focused rhythm where the noise stops, problems untangle, and clarity floods in. Doomscrolling pulls you into anxiety; a relaxed run guides you into Theta. It's the difference between mental panic and mental power—and it's a state you can access intentionally, not just on the road, but in your career and your life.

Doom scrolling vs. Runner Serenity: The Battle for Your Brain

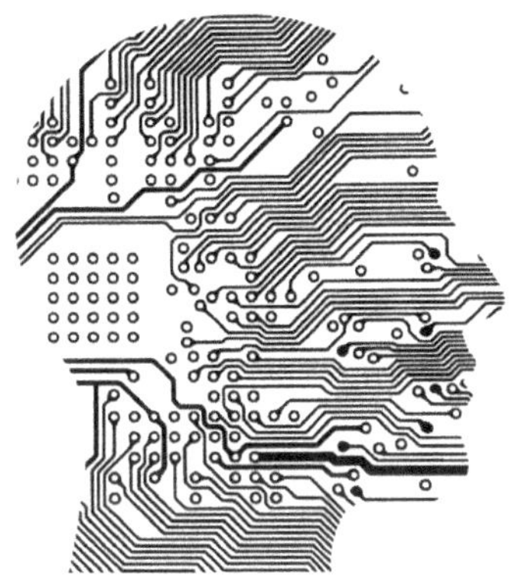

This is what your brain looks like when it's doom scrolling: Your brain is chiefly in high-alert, Beta mode, going into "firefighting" mode. It's designed for problem-solving, sure, but the only problem you're solving when scrolling is which link to click next.

And this? This is what your brain looks like when you're running. You're in Alpha, wakeful relaxation. Maybe even the Theta state—deep relaxation, where solutions bubble up from your subconscious. A focused, calm mind isn't just relaxed; it's creating, it's organizing, and it's making you a better human.

The Ancient Division Tactic, Digitally Enhanced

But here's the kicker: it goes even deeper than our personal screen time. Think about it: have you ever caught yourself starting to avoid, even despise a family member because of their political beliefs? Suddenly, society feels like it's forcing us into two rigid camps, and even worse, we're being subtly led to genuinely despise anyone who doesn't believe exactly like us. It's the ultimate "Us vs. Them" strategy, and frankly, it's working.

This isn't some new, accidental phenomenon. This is the "Divide and Conquer" strategy, a principle as old as empires. Imagine ancient rulers deliberately breaking up a larger, unified populace into smaller, often conflicting groups, simply to maintain their own control. By fostering divisions—whether along ethnic, cultural, or even religious lines—they weakened collective strength, making it far easier to dominate and exploit.

Fast forward to contemporary America, and this ancient strategy has undergone a chilling transformation, thanks to modern technology. What was once a blunt instrument used with broad messaging has become a highly precise and targeted tool for sowing division. Data allows for an unprecedented level of granularity, identifying our personal leanings and feeding us content that reinforces our existing biases, all while demonizing the "other side."

The result? A deeply polarized society. And what this polarization really means is that, once again, you're being USED. Whether its political parties battling for control, cultural identities clashing, economic disparities widening, or even the subtle algorithms that govern our social media feeds, society appears to be in a constant state of fragmentation. But this division isn't accidental—it's a carefully cultivated phenomenon rooted in psychological and philosophical principles, often greasing the wheels for the powerful while leaving Everyday Joe disoriented, disconnected, and feeling isolated.

You might be surprised to learn who's done it before.

Fragmenting for Control: The Roman Art of Disunity

The Roman Republic mastered the "divide and conquer" strategy during its conquest of the Italian Peninsula. Instead of conquering all neighboring city-states and tribes uniformly, Rome made separate treaties and alliances with each one. These agreements often offered slightly different perks or levels of citizenship, and crucially, prevented the allied states from forming their own alliances with each other. This fostered mutual suspicion and competition among the conquered peoples, ensuring they wouldn't unite against Rome.

The Colonizer's Wedge: The British Playbook in India

Perhaps one of the most well-documented examples of "divide and rule" in a colonial context is the British Raj in India. Before the 1857 Indian Rebellion, there was significant cooperation between various religious and ethnic groups, including Hindus and Muslims who fought side-by-side against British rule. Shocked by this unity, the British actively began to foment divisions, particularly between Hindus and Muslims. By fostering these religious and ethnic rivalries, the British weakened any potential united independence movement.

| But is that for a Transformer like You? NO.

Because you, my friend, are different. You understand the insidious nature of this game. You're not just passively consuming the information fed to you; you're actively discerning. You know that true strength lies not in tribalism, but in unity through understanding. You're building a Marathon Mindset, which means you're too focused on your own inner integrity and forward progress to get sidetracked by manufactured feuds.

After all, what do we *really* want?

We all want nice things. We want to feel *better*. We want to be safe, needed, and to know we've got a damn purpose.

Stop the Sprint: Your Brain Deserves a Time Out

This is where we get down to the real work. It starts with a good dose of self-awareness, moves into a nice, deep breath of self-acceptance, and ends with the foundation of self-love. You don't have to be on fire and crush it every single second. It's perfectly okay to have moments of "Meh," because the truth is, your mind doesn't just need sleep, it desperately needs a Time Out.

Think about it like this: when an overactive kid gets a time out, it's not a punishment. It's a strategic move to stop them from escalating into a full-on tantrum. It forces them to stop being overwhelmed by stimulation and gives them a chance to decompress. That's how they find calm. That state of rest for your nervous system isn't just a nice-to-have; it's absolutely non-negotiable. You can't achieve peak performance if you're running on fumes.

This brings up the big question. If there's no easy button, no expensive pill, no doctor's note to reduce all this stress, what do we do? It means we're on our own. It means we have to program the remedy ourselves. We have to be more than intentional. We have to teach our bodies and minds how escape the digital dementia we live in.

Kick Your Ass into Calmness: Mental Detox

Your brain is not a trash can. If you want an epic life, you've got to stop treating your nervous system like a cheap, overcrowded bar. You're overwhelmed because you're addicted to the noise. The answer? The same one you'd give yourself for anything that's gone off the rails: A FULL MENTAL DETOX.

Here's how you shut down the chaos and claim your power:

- If sleeplessness (thank you brain-on-fire anxiety!) is sabotaging your night, do not, under any circumstances, reach for your phone! You're just feeding the beast. Trade that aggressive scrolling for 20 minutes of restorative anything–listening to guided meditation on Calm or Headspace, intentional breathing, watching a Hallmark movie. Whatever it takes to activate your nervous system's calm setting. You need a brake, not more gas!

- That strong urge for an evening drink just to 'switch off'? It's a cheap shortcut. Swap the Chardonnay for a Ritual of Power. Take a hot bath, brew some serious Bergamot tea, or sip a nightcap that gives you a relaxed buzz without the booze, kava-style. Signal to your brain that it's time to be brilliant tomorrow, not just numb tonight.

- Stop letting your inbox hijack your day before you even open your eyes! If you wake up with immediate Gotta-Go Anxiety, resist the urge to check email or the news. Dedicate the first five minutes to slow stretching, or list three things you're currently rejoicing. Set your own pace, and claim your own rewards, don't let the world set them for you.

- If your mind simply won't calm down after hours of work or heavy training, ditch the screen and get tactile. Clean the kitchen, journal by hand, or spend ten minutes building something simple. Engaging your hands forces your hyperactive brain to shut up and pay attention to something real! You family and home will thank you.

- Stop treating your fuel like garbage! If your focus is crashing (or your run fuel is failing you), cut the sugar, fat or soda. Swap them for premium fuel, not panic and pastry crumbs!

In both life and running, your mental operating system requires this strategic intervention. When your mind is running on toxic inputs—constant noise, comparison fatigue, and distraction—you must interrupt the cycle, remove the mental junk, and detox into radical simplicity.

The Vagus Waltz

The stresses of always being "on," of being connected and plugged in, lead to the stimulation of your Sympathetic system. This is the Go, Go, Go System—which is your body's ancient "fight or flight" response, wired to deal with a perceived threat. To find calm, the goal is to remove the focus from this system.

So you ask, "How do I do this, Sensei?"

Well, my little Grasshopper, you do it already and don't even realize it. The key is to actively shift your focus into your Parasympathetic system—the Rest and Reset Button. It's what helps your body recover after a stressful event and promotes relaxation, digestion and sleep.

The key to unlocking this system is the Vagus nerve—the master nerve that controls this calming response. You do it when you take a walk on a sunny day. When you listen to relaxing music with headphones. Even when you hum! The vibrations created by your voice can work like a tiny internal massage for the nerve.

So you've got Your Body's Alarm Bell used to running the show. But we want to shift the focus on Your Body's Chill Pill instead. This is more than switching systems. It's about giving yourself permission to relax. Letting your body know it's safe to unplug. Not only is it safe, it's GOOD for you.

Remember that massage? You know the one. When the massage-maestro was probably an athlete themself. She or he wasn't just a skin pusher, they knew their stuff. They asked questions. They observed how you stood or sat. And then they started. They knew meridians, tested trigger points. Teased fascia. They knew their way around the human body like a Formula 1 driver knows their way around the Las Vegas Grand Prix.

They hit just the right spots. The dense, knotted trapezius in your left shoulder. The searing hamstring that makes your entire leg quiver. The stubborn cramp in your right foot that caused your plantar fascia to seize up and curls your foot like a deformed claw. Each deliberate touch, every minute release of sore muscles, and the intuitive pressure that knew exactly what your body needed.

And then, you were Boneless.

Just as you took control of the Movie of your Life. Just as you accepted responsibility for breaking from the tribe and reprogramming the negative voices – now you take ownership of breaking the archaic pattern of Survival Mode, and moving into Transformer Mode.

This is how we do it.

Rewiring Your Brain (Without a Pricey Gadget)

You've probably seen the ads, right? Those sleek, fancy Vagus nerve stimulator devices—the high-tech headphones or gadgets that promise to send electrical impulses to your brain and magically "chill you out." They cost a pretty penny, and sure, they've got their place in medical treatment for serious stuff like epilepsy or depression.

But here's the absolute best part: you don't need to spend a small fortune to hack your own system. Your body is already equipped with everything you need to decompress, regulate, and tap into your inner calm. It's built right in!

The key is to actively and intentionally stimulate that amazing Vagus nerve – the body's superhighway to relaxation and well-being. And the fastest way to do that?

Breathwork: When your nervous system is going a hundred miles an hour, you don't need a complicated yoga pose or an expensive gadget. You've got the most powerful tool right under your nose: your breath. This one happens to be the most powerful and scientifically backed breathwork technique for stimulating the Vagus nerve–the Physiological Sigh.

This is my go-to "OMG I Need a Minute" technique, and it's totally worth it.

- First, take a big, deep inhale through your nose. Fill your lungs up with air.

- Then, without exhaling, take a second, shorter sip of air. You'll feel your lungs expand just a little bit more. This is the secret sauce.

- Finally, let it all out with a long, satisfying exhale through your mouth. Like you're exhaling a decade's worth of tension.

- That's it. Do that a few times, and your body will get the memo that it's time to hit the reset button. It's an instant de-stressor you can do anywhere—in a meeting, in your car, or in line at the grocery store.

Your Nail Tech is a Neuroscientist

You know that ridiculously amazing, shortie massage your nail lady sneaks in after she's polished your claws? She's not just being nice; she's being a secret, accidental Neuroscience practitioner. That little rub down your neck and the gentle tug on your earlobes? That's her stimulating your Vagus Nerve—the highway that runs straight to your brain's chill button. That incredible feeling isn't a coincidence. It's not just your nails that are rocking; it's your entire nervous system getting a required reset. Get it on– it's the easiest tension release you'll ever find.

Coldplay: The Brain's Nuclear Reset

You want a shortcut to awesome? It's called cold. The sensation of cold is your brain's nuclear restart button, hitting the ultimate 'CTRL+ALT+DEL' on anxiety and stress. Seriously. That's why Peak Performers like actor Mark Wahlberg and leadership guru Robin Sharma don't mess around–they jump into a cold plunge first thing in the morning. It's not about being miserable; it's about making a power move. Cold instantly shuts down the mental noise, shocks your system into hyperfocus, and hands you your clarity back, gift-wrapped.

Good Vibrations: The Nervous System Massage

Check this out! You can also get it done by making noise—Chanting, humming, singing in the car, or even just letting out a big sigh. The vibrations literally give your nervous system a massage. Now it's all making sense why those Gregorian monks would chant and sing. They were blissed out!

Ditch the OMs: Yoga for the Vagus Nerve

Don't roll your eyes at me! You don't need to stand on your head for an hour to get the benefits. Try this: gently bring one ear toward the shoulder or tuck your chin to your chest. Those tiny, gentle stretches release tension in your neck, which is a major pathway for your Vagus nerve. A no-brainer, even for the most yoga-challenged, is the Cat-Cow Pose. Chop chop, on your hands and knees! This simple, rhythmic flow actively massages the organs in your abdomen—another Vagus nerve sweet spot. It's the fastest, easiest way to tell your nervous system to calm the hell down.

Tech-Free Time: Your Ultimate Act of Rebellion

You heard me—put down the damn phone! Tech-free time is your ultimate, non-negotiable act of rebellion against stress, anxiety, and the constant feeling that you should be "doing more." We're not talking about leaving it on silent; we mean putting it in a drawer and walking away for an hour. It's a strategic act of self-preservation. When you cut the digital cord, you stop the energy leak and force your mind to finally catch its breath. This is not downtime; it's a power move.

Go Outside and Get Unplugged

It turns out that the simplest, most accessible, and cheapest method for fixing your brain is just getting out in nature. We overcomplicate everything, but the cure is right outside your door. When you intentionally give yourself a time out and step away from the fluorescent lights and the noise, you're not just finding peace—you're actively and intentionally giving your nervous system the rest it needs. Nature is the original and best prescription for anxiety.

Nature the Great Restorer

There's something almost magical that happens when we step outside, away from all the pings and notifications. The world just... slows down. That endless mental chatter that often accompanies our busy lives starts to fade, replaced by the rhythm of our own breath and the subtle sounds of the natural world. For runners, nature isn't just a pretty backdrop—it's an absolutely essential partner in building and maintaining an indomitable mindset.

Let's explore the science behind how green spaces reduce stress and improve focus. This restoration of mental energy directly translates to overcoming running's inevitable hurdles, cultivating the calm, persistent focus that defines a true Marathon Mindset.

The Walking Philosophers of the Victorian Age

Guess who knew this secret? I know you were thinking runners weren't you? I'm not going to ding you for that. I love that you're onboard! Oddly enough, it's not the hardcore runners, it's folks far more gentile. Imagine the troupe of Downton Abbey on a walking party, not with small talk and parasols, but with deep thought and raw, restorative movement.

Long before modern science, influential thinkers understood this restorative power. The Walking Philosophers of the Victorian Age, such as the Transcendentalists Ralph Waldo Emerson and Henry David Thoreau, recognized a profound truth: putting one foot in front of the other was a sacred, essential practice for both intellectual and spiritual growth.

This movement creates a **Thinking Pace**—fast enough to stimulate blood flow to the brain, yet slow enough for deep reflection and the organization of complex ideas. Philosopher Friedrich Nietzsche, who famously declared, "All truly great thoughts are conceived by walking," found the rhythm of his mountain treks guided his philosophical breakthroughs.

This physical shift is also key to **Breaking Mental Ruts**. When the mind is stuck on a problem, a change of scenery and pace can dislodge stubborn thoughts and reframe difficult questions. Avid urban walker Virginia Woolf used movement as a clear-eyed escape, demonstrating the undeniable power of changing your physical environment to restore mental clarity.

These philosophical pioneers weren't just taking a stroll; they were deliberately engineering their brains for brilliance. Their intuitive practices underscore a timeless lesson now validated by every piece of modern research: unplugging and moving our bodies outdoors isn't a luxury—it's the profound, necessary way we restore and renew the mind. We can learn from the best: if the answer to a complicated problem isn't immediately obvious, the greatest minds in history would simply step outside and let the path guide the answer.

Run The Rhythm, Write The Riff

Let me share one creative cheat code: movement isn't just cardio; it's a high-octane muse. Take the outlaw legend, Willie Nelson. This man has written hundreds of chart-topping songs and performed over 200 albums, all while running a schedule that defined "hard living"—we're talking gallons of whiskey, serious weed, and zero apologies. But here's the secret the world missed: Willie was famous for carving out time to jog and walk long distances. He didn't just use it to burn off the previous night's shenanigans; he used it as a brutal, beautiful mental detox.

The rhythmic repetition of his feet on the asphalt shut down the constant touring chaos, allowing the melodies and the complex lyrics for his next masterpiece—the kind of clarity that gives us the iconic *Georgia on My Mind*—to finally drop in. The road was his writing desk.

Simple Lesson: if movement could transform Willie Nelson's chaos into country gold, imagine what your intentional movement can do for your next big idea. If you're struggling to crack a problem, write that pitch, or land on that killer idea, stop staring at your screen! Your next brilliant breakthrough is waiting for you on the sidewalk.

Can Unplugging Save our Children's Future?

Let's be honest, the statistics are not looking good. We're raising a generation of kids who are constantly plugged in, and it's taking a serious toll on their mental well-being.

A study by the American Psychological Association found that as children's screen time increased, so did their likelihood of developing socio-emotional problems like anxiety and depression.

And the U.S. Surgeon General's research is even more specific, suggesting that adolescents who spend more than three hours a day on social media face double the risk of mental health problems. That's a serious problem, and it's one we all need to be talking about.

SIDEBAR: In June 2024, the University of Glasgow found that children who spent just 60 minutes daily in nature had a 50 percent lower risk of mental health issues. Notably, the benefits were greatest for children from disadvantaged backZgrounds, particularly in terms of improved behavior and social skills.

Maria's Mission: From Classroom to Wildlife Firefighter

Maria Zieja, an ultra runner and former public school teacher, spent 16 years in the classroom before hitting burnout. Holding a master's degree in mathematics education, she sought a new path aligned with her passion for the natural world. This search led her to become a certified Level 1, 2, and 3 nature-based educator through the Association for Nature-Based Education.

The catalyst for this leap of faith was unexpected: during a 50K ultra marathon, Maria saw a sign for a nature school, a concept that was completely new to her. Now, working at Sensory Garden and Play in West Milford, NJ, she views the outdoors as the ultimate classroom, witnessing firsthand the magic of children building confidence, boosting creativity, and thriving through daily nature immersion.

An avid outdoorswoman, Maria has completed ultramarathons from 50K to over 100 miles, in addition to her pursuits of trail running, hiking, and strength training. This deep connection to the land recently compelled her to become a certified wildland firefighter, driven by a desire to directly protect the forests she holds dear. Maria truly is a steward, instilling this responsibility in her students by teaching respect for every creature and modeling small acts of service, like picking up trash on the trail.

Unleashing Potential: Kids, Nature, and Play Redefined

Chantel Zimmerman, founder of Sensory Garden & Play, is spearheading a quiet revolution where education transcends classrooms and leaps into the wild. Her vision is a profound redefinition of early childhood learning, replacing screens and confinement with the curriculum of nature: direct play, boundless exploration, and a visceral connection to the natural world.

The COVID-19 pandemic unexpectedly accelerated this movement, establishing the outdoors as a safe, vital catalyst for engagement and well-being. However, Zimmerman recognized a critical disparity: many inner-city children lacked fundamental access to safe green spaces. This conviction led to the creation of the non-profit division, committed to providing equitable access to the transformative power of nature.

For children whose nervous systems are perpetually attuned to the anxieties and vigilance of urban environments, the outdoor shift is profound. Initially fearful, they consistently leave the Sensory Garden & Play environment with a new refrain: "I feel so peaceful." This powerful testimony highlights nature's ability to regulate and calm, replacing a heightened state of awareness with serenity.

Chantel's teaching philosophy is built on purposeful connection, rooted in the question she asks her students: "How is your heart?" This empathetic approach informs her education, challenging the conventional wisdom of teaching subjects like insects or weather indoors when their natural habitat is just outside. Her broader vision—encompassing educational cohorts and dedicated spaces for children with disabilities—is driven by an unwavering belief in nature's power to shape the future.

Escape to the Country–Unlocking Leadership Through Nature

It isn't just the educational world that's embracing nature's profound impact; countless companies are now seeking experts to help their valued employees decompress, recalibrate, and grow. One company doing this is Get the Edge UK, led by visionaries Lisa and Jon Davies. As a sales, management, and leadership development company they emphasize, "We believe that stepping into nature isn't just rejuvenating; it's transformational leadership development."

This deep conviction is precisely why Get the Edge UK's impactful retreats take place at Hill Holt Wood, an award-winning social enterprise nestled in 34 acres of ancient woodland in the UK. This place is so much more than a venue; it becomes a living classroom, alive with purpose. It offers alternative education for young people, supportive learning for adults, and crucially, for these leadership programs.

When leaders join these retreats, immersed in the dappled light, breathing the rich earth, and enveloped by the subtle hum of forest life, the shift in their energy is palpable. Guided by Lisa and her team of experts, phones go silent, and minds open. In that newfound calm, the sessions dive deep into how the mind truly works, exploring how our thoughts shape our physiology and performance. Participants are guided through carefully crafted, embodied experiences, so they can feel firsthand how energy influences every interaction, every decision, and every relationship.

Leaders reconfigure their internal antenna: a clearer mind, a steadier breath, and a more spacious presence emerges. They begin to intuitively understand how their inner state—their personal energy—ripples out, either activating or depleting the energy of those they lead. They return to their organizations not just with new leadership tools, but with a reset nervous system, renewed clarity, deeper connection, and a keener sense of their impact.

Your Pathway to Restoration

You know the trail. It's barely noticeable. It looks like a deer path, untrodden and barely visible. But its quiet invitation calls to you. So you take it. Again and again. With each deliberate footfall, you press down the wild grasses, coaxing the shrubs aside, until that subtle whisper becomes a clear, viable path. It grows grooved and intimate, comfortable under your steady footsteps.

This pathway? It didn't exist for you before. Maybe a few wild things knew it – whitetail deer, maybe a stray coyote, but humans? Nope. Now it's uniquely yours. You didn't just walk that path; you *created* it.

And this, my friend, is precisely how you forge a Marathon Mindset. You are actively creating a brand-new neural pathway in your brain—one that consistently leads to calm, clarity, and unshakeable strength. All it takes is the courageous choice to step onto it, again and again, even when the old, well-worn roads of stress and distraction call louder.

You're not just taking a stroll; you're rewiring your magnificent brain. You're gently, firmly, teaching your nervous system that it doesn't need to be on high alert 24/7. You're learning that the "little things" you've blown out of proportion don't matter so much in the grand scheme. What truly matters are your personal autonomy, your radiant peace, and your vibrant vitality. The moment you start trusting—trusting yourself, trusting your perfectly imperfect choices—everything begins to flow with exhilarating ease.

External Validation: Ditch the Audience

This shift truly ignites when you stop clinging to external validation like it's a life raft. When you finally, deeply accept that you have chosen, and chosen well. There's no audience to appease, no tired character to perform. And who are you when absolutely nobody is watching? If that reflection doesn't spark joy, then yeah, you're going to keep frantically searching outside yourself for answers.

But here's the secret: You can't hide from your authentic self. You can only choose to accept it. And embrace it. And finally realize, with unshakable clarity, that you are here to be unapologetically YOU. The sooner you step into that truth, the sooner you feel the profound release of genuine peace and decompression. That, my darling, is the ultimate gift of unplugging. You simply don't need anyone's approval, their little hearts, or their fleeting validation. Your worth is an inside job, and it's already complete.

| It's Ok Not to Panic

Oh, the pressure cooker! We pile it on ourselves, don't we? "I have to nail this presentation." "I must book those fencing lessons for the kids ASAP." "Why on earth did they skip recycling this week?!" Our minds have a tendency to go on a frantic hunt for everything that's wrong. It's like a hyper-vigilant lighthouse, endlessly sweeping its beam across the horizon, fixated on every potential shipwreck, every tiny flicker of trouble. Because, let's be honest, that frenzied scanning has become its twisted comfort zone. But here's the drastic truth: the only thing we need to do is just be here, fully and vibrantly, in this very moment.

Lessons from a Three-Legged Zen Master

You might find this hard to believe, but the best teacher I ever had about staying in the moment was our dog, Sonny. Because he HAD to. He was discovered wandering the streets of Texas with his front right leg hanging off. A no-kill shelter took him in, amputated the limb and rehabbed him for a new home.

Wayne found him online a month before Covid. "I have a premonition that we need a dog." He prophesied. It had been two years since we had a dog, we felt ready. Wayne showed me a picture of a beautiful red cattle dog mix, a tripod, smiling into the camera. A real smile. A smile that said, yeah, it's been tough but hey! I'm doing ok.

"I have to meet this dog," Wayne mused. "Could he really be this happy after all he's endured?"

Yes he could. Sonny was a living lesson in humility, turning out to be a master of the present moment. He didn't just forget his trauma; he chose to live in a constant state of unwavering appreciation. No complaints. No 'my phantom limb aches.' Just a wagging tail and soft whimpers that greeted us every morning. He devoured food, anything! Dry kibble, carrot sticks, even ice! He patiently waited for his morning walk and lived for a drive in the car. He even had his own Instagram: Tripod Foodie, and trust me, it got a hell of a lot more action than mine did! People loved his story and rooted for the boy who finally belonged to a family pack. He had found his people, and he finally knew what it felt to be safe and loved for five incredible years.

So, it was a shock when he suddenly had a hard time moving. He couldn't walk, couldn't see, he took long naps. I took him driving because he still loved to be in motion. I was crying, mourning what I suspected was to come. It was in the rearview mirror, as I cried, that I caught his eye. The message came through, loud and clear: "Mama, it's okay. Stay right here. This moment is perfect."

Now I know all you pet owners out there know what I'm talking about. Your fur babies speak to you all the time, no? Sometimes they vocalize, but more often it's in their eyes, unspoken energy, their body language. They are perfectly able to convey messages and emotions. Somehow, while we humans struggle to communicate with **each other**, animals have mastered the art of talking straight to the soul.

Sonny repeated his message for several weeks as his health declined. "Stay in this moment, Mama. It's perfect." And it was! I was entwined in the magic of this dog overflowing with love for family, his home, and the world in that moment.

Even when the vet gave us the verdict – a brain tumor. Even when he couldn't walk, much less stand. Even when he ate chocolate kisses for the first time, just before he got the blue injection that would close his eyes forever. Every single one of those moments was perfect.

I still hear his message, especially when I'm driving and peek in the rearview mirror, expecting to see my Corgi-faced boy. I'll be sobbing and remember his parting gift.

So I bestow it to you, my friend. This moment right now. This moment is perfect, isn't it? You are safe. There's no wave that's going to drown you. No fire crackling at the door. No illness that can consume you. Right now you are safe. And if you're not, then I wish you Godspeed to safety.

For most of us, the present moment is a fortress of safety. No need to chew on the disappointing past. No need to stress about projections for the future. Just here, right now, is your sanctuary. Close your eyes, let your shoulders drop, and exhale the worry out of your soul.

Altar of Overwhelm

Several years ago, when I was consulting for the glitzy world of luxury travel, I worked with some seriously sharp people. We'd brainstorm as a team – Data, Technology, Customer Experience, Organization and Process. Sometimes, a task would pop up that didn't fit neatly into any area of expertise. That's when the Brit on our team would chime in with the most reassuring words you could ever hear: "I'll take care of that. Leave it with me."

Total relief.

Imagine if you had a place—a metaphorical Altar of Overwhelm—where you could just ditch all the soul-sucking, mind-numbing, paralyzing crap that's been bogging you down. That endlessly growing to-do list that stares at you like a judgment-filled monster? Leave it. That passive-aggressive text thread with your family that's stealing your joy? Leave it. The incessant worry about whether you're "enough" or doing "enough" or being enough in this unpredictable world? Release that suffocating weight.

Here's the cosmic punchline: When you actually engage and commit to doing the work—to harnessing the incredible tools that are already sitting inside your magnificent self—you absolutely, positively, without a shadow of a doubt, gain the power to leave that heavy baggage behind.

So, what are you ready to release at the Altar of Overwhelm?

- The nagging guilt over that pile of laundry threatening to become sentient?
- The constant low hum of financial anxiety keeping you up at 3 AM?
- That looming work project that feels less like a task and more like an existential threat?
- The dread of your brand's digital visibility disappearing overnight thanks to some inscrutable algorithm change?
- The worry about your daughter's college applications, your son's messy room, or your dog's questionable breath?

This isn't about ignoring your responsibilities; it's about reclaiming your power over the mental clutter. It's about recognizing that you don't have to carry every single burden, every single worry, every single "what if." You have the agency to decide what stays with you and what gets dropped like a hot potato at the Altar of Overwhelm.

Do you know why? Because you are not built to be a walking trash compactor for every stray anxiety and ridiculous "should" that floats by. The profound relief you're seeking isn't hiding outside yourself; it's waiting for you the second you stop carrying other people's crap. You deserve that glorious feeling of letting go. So take a deep breath, mentally drop that laundry, that debt, that digital dread right at the Altar of Overwhelm.

Rules of the Road

- You get a Finisher Medal for learning how our tech-driven society is wired for Stress

- You yanked back the curtain on the mental health crisis plaguing our digitally-overloaded world.

- You hit a nerve by understanding the Vagus Waltz – The magical chill pill.

- You delved into the secret great American thinkers knew – walking baby!

- You unearthed the antidote to our modern madness: Unplugging isn't just for young people; it benefits all ages.

- You discovered a simple, powerful truth: just one hour in nature can cut the risk of mental health issues in half.

- You met people on a mission to transform the great outdoors into the ultimate classroom and boardroom.

- You heard the Zen Dog's message to Stay in the Moment.

- You left your worries at the Altar of Overwhelm.

Now that we've seen how stepping away can reset even the most seasoned leaders, let's take that energy and refocus it inward. How is your movie—progressing? Are you hitting any roadblocks, or are you ready to jump into the next scene?

CHAPTER 8

CRACKING THE CODE – MENTAL MASTERY

So, how's your movie going?

Did your director take a hard left, hijacking the script with shocking plot twists you never saw coming? Is your star performer AWOL, lost in a tempest of doubt? Or worse, is your leading lady chugging White Claws in an unlit apartment after getting unceremoniously dumped?

If any of that hit a little too close to home, it's time to yank that remote control back. Because you aren't here to just watch the movie version of yourself; you're in the thrilling, messy, but essential process of becoming the better, bolder, more magnificent SELF you were meant to be. Call it your Future Self, your Higher Self, your Inner Superstar—whatever lights your fire. But know this: you have to take action to transform. That means consciously evolving into a person who is truly aligned with your deepest desires.

You're a genius at navigating the external world, aren't you? Paying bills online with lightning speed? Check. Venmo-ing cash to your grandkid across the country? Double check. Snagging an 80% discount on meds? Thank you, Mark Cuban.

But here's the million-dollar question: Do you know how to connect with the fierce, brilliant, unstoppable divinity that lives within you? Because that's the power source, baby! That's when the universe starts doing your bidding and you don't just combat negativity—you transcend it.

We talked about nature's soul-restoring power in the last chapter. Now? It's time to get down to the unapologetic nitty-gritty of taking absolute ownership over that pesky dragon of negativity. It's more than just taming that bad boy. It's about transfiguring into the Human Being you've always wanted to become—the one who is the unshakeable master of their mind. And when you do that, guess what, my wizard? You'll hold the magic wand forever, finding unwavering control right there in your own glorious head.

Let's dive in.

Discovering Your Northstar: Your Goal

Finding your goal isn't rocket science, it's the ignition key to your entire life. It's the moment your potential roars to life because you finally have a clear destination. Every great act, every lasting transformation, starts with a goal.

This Northstar is more than just an outcome; it's the purpose that drives you. It's the reason you wake up early, the reason you say "No" to distractions, and the reason you put in the uncomfortable, sometimes tedious work. This purpose—this vision of who you are about to become—deserves to be epic.

And if a crystal-clear sense of purpose had a theme song, what would it be? It wouldn't be some sad, slow ballad about wishing things were different. It would be a fierce declaration of intent, a punchy anthem demanding your best effort. That's right, your purpose gives you Eye of the Tiger.

Maybe it's not a race, but a ruthless climb to the top of your field. It's the entrepreneur who declares, "I will land that eight-figure client and build an empire!" It's the student who, staring down a mountain of textbooks, swears, "I will nail a perfect 4.0 this semester!" It's the determined individual who, feeling the quiet weight of their body, commits, "I will lose these twenty pounds and finally feel at home in my own skin."

A goal is not a suggestion; it is a sacred contract with your future self. Without a specific goal, your raw ambition is just a fire with nowhere to go. It burns bright for a second and then fizzles into a pathetic pile of self-doubt. But a real goal? It channels your magnificent flame, directing every ounce of your precious energy toward a powerful, specific outcome.

Think about some of the world's most epic goals:

- To accelerate the world's transition to sustainable energy – **Tesla**
- To inspire and nurture the human spirit, one person, one cup, and one neighborhood at a time – **Starbucks**
- To give ordinary folks the chance to buy the same things as rich people – **Walmart**

At the end of the day, the real victory isn't just checking off a box. It's about a relentless, lifelong pursuit of becoming a fully realized human being–someone who is not just winning at a single objective, but winning at the art of living itself. It's the daily, deliberate act of becoming well-rounded, elevated, loving and deeply fulfilled person. Now that's triumph.

What is your goal? Write it down now on a piece of paper. Hang on to that piece of paper. We'll work with it later.

You Are the Damn Signal

Right this very second, whether you're chugging coffee at your desk or waiting in line, you're not just existing—you are BROADCASTING. You are a walking, breathing transmitter, and every thought, every feeling, every worry, and every ounce of love you exude is a signal jetting into the world.

And the universe? It's a giant, screaming echo chamber. It will send that exact signal straight back to you.

The simple, brutal truth is this: It's not about how badly you want something. It's about the energy you are projecting. You can wish for a promotion all you want, but if you're a churning ball of anger and desperation, muttering, "It's about time I got it, dammit! I'm more qualified than anyone!"—that tense energy isn't just inside you. It's a palpable force field radiating from you. It's the emotional equivalent of Pig-Pen's perpetual dust cloud—a thick, undeniable, and frankly, off-putting aura that announces your arrival before you even speak.

This is the Law of Attraction, darling. Your mind isn't a container; it's a powerful broadcasting station. The frequency you radiate—your thoughts, feelings, and deepest convictions—is what the universe tunes into. When you feel dim and grim, you're asking for more dimness and grimness. Period.

The Vibe Shift That Saved My Ass

Years ago, I had a health crisis that landed me squarely in the emergency room of panic. Tests indicated cysts. My doctor, with the detached cruelty of a scientist observing a specimen, deduced it was cancer. I was terrified. Not only was my future suddenly wiped clean of children, but my very life felt at stake.

When I told my mother, I expected tears, panic, maybe a fainting spell. Instead, I got silence. And then she laid down the law: "Never let anyone tell you that you're sick."

I was initially baffled. But then, the Hallelujah Chorus started playing in my head: *Hang on now. I'm a Reiki Master. I help people bring their bodies back into balance all the time. Why the hell am I not doing this for myself?*

I realized my focus was screwed up. Focusing on "getting better" or "finding a cure" reeked of the state of dis-ease, the ultimate separation from health. That was the wrong frequency.

So, I shifted the signal. I created a new, non-negotiable narrative: I am perfectly well. Right NOW. I didn't picture a slow recovery; I pictured myself vibrant, healthy, pulsing with life—a done deal. I visualized myself playing tennis in the warm sun, hitting effortless groundstrokes. I saw myself gliding through city streets jammed with traffic, smiling cheekily at my fellow commuters.

I did this for weeks, focusing only on the feeling of thriving.

When I finally found a new doctor who looked at the films, she simply said, "You're fine. This is not cancer; these are just peri-menopausal cysts. They'll go away."

Oh! Sweet mystery of life–at last I've found you! Life and death in one month. I'm telling you, you do not appreciate your fabulous life until you're about to lose it. The biggest takeaway wasn't just the relief; it was the confirmation that my internal broadcast—that quiet, confident frequency of alignment—is the most potent force in the Universe.

Two Critical Lessons Learned:

1.   Listen to your Mother!

2. Stop Chasing. Start Being.

The Universe Responds to Your Energy, Not Your Desperation

Let's talk about the ultimate celestial punchline, beloved: You don't attract what you **Want**, You attract what you **Are**.

You want to feel more joy? Go unleash it. You want to feel more victorious? Start acting like the champion you were born to be. The moment you start thinking and acting like the person who already has that raise, that incredible relationship, or that ridiculously rocking body, the universe has no choice but to deliver it.

Why? Because the universe responds to authority, not desperation. Because your energetic frequency is no longer a wish; it's a command, and the universe is wired to comply.

And I know what you're thinking.

- How the hell do I project 'CEO energy' when I'm fielding customer support calls from my tiny kitchen and hoping my roommate doesn't walk in?

- How do I radiate 'vibrant health' when my damn knees ache going up the stairs and my favorite jeans haven't fit in three years?

- How do I act like I deserve a soulmate when I just got ghosted by someone whose profile picture was a dog wearing a hat?

Believe me, I get it. It's a cosmic conundrum. And it's draining you faster than a phone with every app running at once. But here's the deal: that's the whole damn point of this book. We're here to uncover the truths that have been hidden in plain sight, to disrupt the tired, old crap that's been blocking your light, and to finally claim your absolute birthright of joy and success. But you must choose to upgrade.

The Whisper of a Miracle: All it Takes Is One Nice Thought

Listen up, because this is a game-changer straight from a cosmic luminary like Esther Hicks. Just one single, sparkly thought can flip the script on your whole friggin' day. I am not kidding. Try it right now. Think of one sweet idea. Let it tickle a crevice of your mind. A good feeling, a tiny moment of sweetness, can instantly start carving a new path.

Do it. Now.

What's a tiny little win you had today? Maybe you were in the elevator and you complimented the woman wearing a chic red suit. Turns out, she's the new CMO, and she was totally blown away by your vibe. She loved your energy, your communication skills, the way you carry yourself. Now, don't just let that go. Spin that sucker in your fantasy! See yourself getting called into her office. Hear her tell you that you've got exactly the kind of energy her team needs. Visualize her asking you to meet the rest of her team. Oh, and how do you feel about attending a conference in Zurich?

It's not about monumental triumphs yet. It's about that hole-in-one you hit on the golf course, the killer dress you found on the clearance rack, or the genuine smile you got from the crossing guard this morning. One nice thought is a tiny, powerful seed. You plant it, and it blossoms into a wispy tree. Nurture it like it was a precious child, because it is.

The Billion-Dollar Secret They Kept From You

There are secrets that used to be heavily guarded by the mystery schools, dating back thousands of years. We're talking ancient wisdom, folks, the kind that was whispered in hushed tones and protected like gold. And one of those secrets is mind-blowing in its simplicity and utterly profound in its power: Your mind doesn't know the difference between what's vibrantly imagined, and what's real.

The mind's internal theater is so convincing, it can't distinguish between a compelling mental rehearsal and an external, lived experience.

Think about it. Why do we flinch when we watch a scary movie, even though we know it's just actors on a green screen? Why does your heart pound when you envision giving a big speech, even if you're just sitting in your pajamas? It's because your brain, bless its literal heart, processes these mental rehearsals as if they're happening right now. It doesn't have a "real" or "fake" button for your thoughts. It just responds to the emotions and sensations you conjure.

This isn't some arcane spiritual rhetoric; modern neuroscience is plugging this from podcasts to dissertations. When you visualize, certain neural pathways light up, strengthening the very connections you'd use if you were actually performing the action. So, when you dwell on worst-case scenarios, your brain is literally practicing anxiety. But when you immerse yourself in visions of triumph, confidence, and sheer joy? You're building superhighways for success!

Here's the billion-dollar question: if your brain literally can't tell the difference between what's vividly imagined and what's real, why in the hell would you waste a single second filling it with garbage? Why would you choose to marinate your mind in a crockpot of violence, anxiety, and shameless mis-truths that lead straight to a tidal wave of negativity?

Don't Obsess on the Subway Rat

I've been riding the New York Subway for 38 years, and back in the '80s, the tunnels were a straight-up disaster movie. There was this river of greasy, black water sloshing under the rails, and rats—and I mean giant, swaggering rats—scampering through the grimy sludge, feasting on discarded potato chip bags and candy wrappers.

I'd find myself staring, totally grossed out but still morbidly fascinated. Until one day, it hit me: Why was I looking at the nastiest thing in this whole damn subway? Just down the platform, Leo the saxophone guy was wailing out "Funkytown," and the walls were covered in bizarrely colorful art. Why in the hell was I letting my mind obsess over a rat when there was a full-blown concert and a pop-art gallery right in front of me?

Every single moment you spend dwelling on a negative emotion or thought, you're literally rewiring your brain for misery. You're not just idly thinking; you're actively practicing a life you absolutely do not want. Wouldn't it make a lot more sense to relentlessly flood your mind with bold, breathtaking visions of your ultimate, fully-realized self? To shower your brain with delightful daydreams of doing fabulous things, feeling vibrantly alive, and gushing with love?

Of course it does.

THIS is Mental Mastery. It's about being the alchemist of your own mind. Just like the ancient mystics turned lead into gold, you have the power to take your 'base' nature—the negativity, the fear, the ignorance—and transmute it into the gorgeous, pure gold of enlightenment and unstoppable wisdom. This is a systematic process of purging old beliefs and cultivating new insights, aimed at transforming your inner landscape from a battlefield into a vibrant kingdom.

The best part? You don't have to do it alone. There are disciplines that will make you an unstoppable force. Let's bring out the big guns.

The Monitor of Your Mind

Let's kick things off with a little experiment. Remember that juicy goal of yours? Now, write it down where you can see it every single day. Slap it on a sticky note on your laptop, set a 7 a.m. calendar notification, or scrawl it in your journal. Get it out of your head and into the world, making it real, undeniable, and impossible to ignore.

Remember those wild daydreams you used to have as a kid? Staring out the window, playing out fantasies in your head, picturing yourself doing mind-blowing, impossible things? You thought you were just fantasizing, but in fact, you were rewiring your brain with a brand-new schematic. My grand fantasy was winning Wimbledon at sixteen. Now, obviously, I'm not a grand slam champion, but watching Tracy Austin do it proved that audacious dreams aren't just for a lucky few.

The importance of imagination cannot be overstated: when you saturate your mind with visions of wonderful things unfolding, when you allow yourself to truly expect greatness in your journey, it stops being magic and becomes a blueprint for reality.

The Elite Runner's Secret: Pre-Program Victory

Elite athletes know that the true race is won long before the starting gun fires; it's won in the brilliant, relentless theater of the mind.

Just look at Eliud Kipchoge, the man who shattered the human barrier and proved that a sub two-hour marathon wasn't just possible, it was inevitable. He achieved this through a ruthless, disciplined mastery of his inner world—a mastery rooted in visualization. Before every race, Kipchoge would spend time locked in his mind, running the course over and over again. He didn't just see the turns; he felt the rhythm, heard the cheers, and saw himself crossing that finish line in a blaze of glory.

This wasn't a wish; it was a mental blueprint for victory, a confidence-building rehearsal that made the impossible feel like a done deal.

Runners use this technique to outsmart their inner critic and overcome real-world obstacles. Mark Plaatjes, for instance, extensively practiced visualization before his gold-medal marathon at the 1993 World Championships. He "ran" every possible scenario, every hill, and every potential problem so vividly in his mind that when the actual race unfolded, he was prepared for anything.

This is the power of pre-programming your brain for success. By visualizing the precise sights, sounds, and even the feeling of your heart rate accelerating, you train yourself to stay calm, collected, and to execute your plan perfectly, even in the most chaotic environment. You are not just fantasizing; you are actively conducting a high-stakes, zero-risk mental rehearsal.

The 4-Step Manifestation Plan

Let's get down to the actionable plan. I want you to make that goal a reality, one step at a time. So guess what? I created a formula, not as mind blowing as Einstein's, but pretty good for a little ole mortal. The most powerful form of manifestation isn't a passive wish; it's an active, energetic alignment. This formula reframes the process, turning a simple desire into an inevitable reality.

Grab a comfy chair, close your eyes, and let's go.

Step 1: Calm the Mind

The KEY is to first soothe your nervous system. Before you can take transformative action, you must shift your body and mind into a calm, tranquil state. Anxiety, chaos, and distraction are symptoms of survival mode—a state where you can only fight or flee, not actively create your reality.

The Alignment Breath

Take a deep, soul-clearing breath. Take a breath like you're filling your lungs with the freshest, most restorative air in the world—air filtered by mountain peaks and washed by the quiet sea. It is cool. It is soothing.

Feel this cool air begin its gentle wash over your entire being. Start at your hot head, allowing the tension around your temples to soften. Let the breath flow down your tight throat, releasing all the unsaid words and the pressure held there. It slides past your stiff neck and shoulders, shedding the weight of your day, one muscle fiber at a time. The breath flutters past your heart, which may be thundering at first, but then settles into a calm, steady drum.

As this breath reaches the base of your abdomen, pause. Hold the stillness for just a moment, recognizing this pocket of serenity you've intentionally created.

Feeling more peaceful, my chickadee?

Step 2: Visualize the Scene on the Monitor of Your Mind

Now I want you to engage all your senses: What does your dream goal look like? What sounds do you hear? What does it feel like to touch the object or walk in that space? What do you smell? Let's dive into the vivid details of your goal. Play it out so you can see it on the monitor of your mind. Close your eyes and see yourself in the moment. The thing, person, state you intensely desire. See it happening.

And because it's your monitor and your mind, guess what you hold in your warm, tender hands? The Remote Control. That's right. You get to hit pause on the scene of you thanking the Committee for appointing you to the Board, and hit replay. Of you, glowing as you share the news with your family and friends. Of you, gleeful as you see your bank account, your 401k hit $5.3 million.

Oh, wait, you've also got a button for slow motion. See yourself at dinner, looking dashing with your long desired flame at the opening of a hot new restaurant. Slow down the scene so you can see every glowy, radiant inch of your sunbathed face as you soak in the rays on your honeymoon. Slo Mo as you watch yourself hit the winning golf swing, the arch of your back fierce and powerful. Slow down the reel of you crossing the finish line of a race, sweaty, exhausted, triumphant.

You see, visualization can be as exciting and creatively unique as each individual. Enter Dr. David Hamilton, a Kindness Scientist. Isn't that the coolest title you've ever heard? He's taking a cue from the mystery schools and dishing the truth about how to use ancient techniques to achieve your goals. He calls it: "A better you. Backed by Science". Let's take the case of weight loss. In his blog "How to Think yourself Slim" he shares a story about a woman who used an astonishing visualization technique. She imagined Pac Man-like creatures eating away fat. Chomp chomp chomp. After 5 months she dropped 21 pounds. How's that for gaming success?!

You see, it's your movie, and it can be as unique and authentic as only you can be. So, pump up that imagination, play with the symbols and hidden codes that bring meaning to only you. Coax out your inner Walter Mitty dreamer. Whatever drives you, makes you giggle, sizzle, brings you pleasure, makes your eyes glaze in reward. Use them to fantasize your dream happening.

Mental Rehearsal: The Ultimate Cheat Code

Think about it: elite athletes, coaches, and even your friend who just crushed her first 10k all know the ultimate cheat code to greatness. Mental rehearsal isn't just as good as the real thing; it's a quantum leap forward. It's the secret weapon of champions.

Celebrated swimmer Michael Phelps (you know the guy who won 28 Olympic medals) worked with his coach, Bob Bowman, to develop a unique and detailed visualization routine. He would sit quietly and mentally visualize a perfect video of his race from start to finish. He'd feel the cool water, hear the roar of the crowd, and time every stroke, kick, and turn. This mental reel was so precise that he would even visualize potential disasters, like his goggles filling with water, and rehearse his reaction—swimming on regardless, counting strokes in the dark. This wasn't about wishing for victory; it was about meticulously rehearsing every sensory detail of success, creating a mental blueprint that his body knew how to follow.

The payoff is just as profound when you rehearse it mentally, as when you do it physically

This isn't just for Olympic athletes; it's for everyone. A concert pianist doesn't just practice scales; she closes her eyes and feels the intricate dance of her fingers across the keys, hears the lyrical precision of each note, expresses the emotion from one movement to the next. A tennis star doesn't just hit serves; he mentally rehearses the fluid motion, the snap of the wrist, the ball spinning perfectly inside the line. A golfer doesn't just stand over the ball; she sees the perfect arc, the satisfying thud of the club, and the ball dropping into the cup.

Here's the cosmic punchline: Your magnificent mind doesn't know the difference between what you're vividly conjuring and what's happening outside your body. The payoff is just as valuable when you rehearse it mentally, as when you do it physically. Just as your muscles grow stronger when you lift weights, your mind strengthens the very neural pathways you'll use when you run, firing the same neurons as if your feet were hitting the pavement. It's building the muscle memory and strengthening the neural superhighways for success.

Jack Nicklaus famously emphasized the mental aspect of golf with his quote:

"The game of golf is 90% mental and 10% physical."

Step 3. Unleash the Feelings

This is the secret sauce. How does it feel when you achieve your goal? Is it pure excitement? Unstoppable joy? A quiet sense of calm accomplishment? Redemption? Saturate yourself in the feeling of reaching that goal. Feel it in your bones, in your breath, in your soul.

Now, this is a crucial step. It is the act of living and breathing the reality of your desire before it has physically appeared. You must shift your identity to become the person who already has what you want. How would the person who already has their goal feel, think, act and talk?

Speaking of talking, do me a favor. Go ahead and say your dream out loud. Don't just whisper it like you're afraid someone might judge you. Say it so your ears, your mind and heart feel the vibration of faith surging inside you. You don't have to prove to God that you're worthy of your dream. You have to prove it to yourself.

Worthy of Your Dreams

So, let me ask you this: How would the person who already has that colossal goal feel, think, speak, and act? Would a Sales virtuoso who just closed a killer, eight-figure deal snap at their kids for putting the spoons in the wrong drawer? Would an athlete who just landed a million-dollar endorsement deal lose their mind because there are three open salads in the fridge? A person with a healthy command of their body wouldn't bitch at their dog for a 6 AM walk in the freezing rain, would they? They know the victory is already locked and loaded. These silly little incidents? They're minor trifles, tiny specks of cosmic dust in the grand scheme of things.

You Are the Soulmate You've Been Waiting For

Listen, I've been right there in the trenches with you. I know what it's like to yearn for recognition, going to a wedding with a gal pal, what it's like to desire love. Matter of fact, my hubby and I met on Match.com. He was divorced after 24 years and I was blindsided by the abrupt end of an engagement. One thing I know, when things go wrong it's never the other person. It's always about YOU. I went on a quest for ultimate, gut-punching truths. What makes a person the target of divine, adoring relationships? Why were some women blissfully married, while others (hot bodies, C-Suite positions and luxury cars) remain unhappy, unattached and searching for love like it was a hidden treasure?

So, I became a detective of love. I devoured books, hit every workshop, intense dating clinics, and weekend retreats. I researched, chatted, and went on enough dates to fill the Yellow Pages. And here's what I learned: Nobody wants to join a pity-party cruise. People are magnetically pulled towards contented and happy people. They don't want to hear the sob story about how you got deserted or how miserable your life is without a partner. They want to be around someone who is celebrating their own life.

It's not about being an "OMG, I'm so into myself" narcissist. It's simpler than that. It's about a deep, quiet, unwavering belief that you know who you are, and you embrace that person. You love yourself and your life. When you don't, no amount of posturing, breathless tales of the old Palladium clubbing days, Hamptons shore houses, or New Year Eve's countdowns at Windows of the World can hide your discontent. It's just you and your quivering heart.

Energetic Signature

And all this boils down to the energy you project. I was enjoying my life; my home, my adorable garden. I was playing tennis, taking my dog to the park, street fairs on the upper west side and on road trips. I cooked exquisite meals, listened to music and danced, I even invented cocktails, (Tequito was my inspired concoction – mojito with tequila, instead of rum.) And you know what? I was enough, just as I was. The dog might have thought I was batshit crazy, but sometimes he joined in the frolics. I was happy with me. And that energy showed. My tagline on Match was: Are You an Adventurous Companion? I was inviting a guy to be my companion in the things I loved to do. And in the meantime, I had fun being me.

And it worked. I attracted a man who was looking for the same things I was. More importantly, he was aligned to the same energy I was emitting.

You don't have to speak Japanese, you don't have to be a concerto soloist, or even run your own hedge fund. But you do have to like yourself, and your life. Otherwise, why would anyone want to join you there?

This is why you have to become your OWN soulmate. You have to proclaim to the world, and yourself – I am worthy of Love!!! All of this becomes your energetic signature. And *that* Cherie, is your authentic, nobody else got it blueprint. It's what you've been working on your entire life. The thing that makes you blood and guts, lace and bones YOU.

| Become the Person Worthy of Your Dreams

My friends saw my success online and asked for advice. I asked them the only question that matters: *What do you want to feel like when you're with him?* Some were befuddled. Some had never thought about it before. Some said: what does that have to do with anything?

Well, my darling dingbat, it has everything to do with it. How can you attract love when you don't even know what it feels like?

So tell me, what does it FEEL like when you have your dream, your goal, your desire?

Saturate yourself in that feeling. Enrobe yourself with it. Feel the energy surge through you. Let it ignite your entire being. Don't just see the action; feel the thrill of success. How does it FEEL to know you hit your financial goal? How does it feel to find the partner of your dreams? Drench yourself in the sensations. Because those sensations will attract the thing you desire. You have to embody what you desire. And THAT will attract it to you.

Celebrate Your Victory

Now that you've sent your clear, aligned signal, it's time to cash the check. I want you to celebrate the absolute fulfillment of your dream like it happened five minutes ago. Don't wait until you cross the finish line— celebrate the non-negotiable fact that you already have. Your brain is now officially practicing success.

Feel the confetti raining down on you. I'm talking full-body, high-definition, unapologetic success. Is it the new corner office? Feel the rich leather of the chair. Is it the marathon medal? Hear the roar of the crowd and feel the cool, heavy weight of the hardware around your neck. This isn't some fluffy fantasy; it's a psychological blueprint. When you feel that visceral rush of success, your brain officially registers it as a done deal.

But the biggest party trick, the move that keeps the abundance flowing like champagne at a launch party? Gratitude.

Gratitude isn't a meek, polite thank you. It's an energetic force—it fires a laser beam of pure, unadulterated joy into the atmosphere. It instantly shifts your broadcast from "I hope to get this" to "I already have this." Be grateful for the courage you already had to start. Be grateful for the lessons the Universe has already sent you. Be grateful for the money you have, not the money you need.

You know what I like to say? *Thank you, I'll have more.*

Your Inner Spotlight

For his 59th birthday Wayne treated himself to a Porsche Macan in Gentian blue. We had never seen that sapphire color before and it was stunning! Soon we started seeing the exact same car everywhere on the road. It was like we were magnets for other electric blue Macans.

Your brain has this amazing filter called the Reticular Activating System (RAS). It's like your personal spotlight, drawing your attention to whatever you're focused on. This is why you suddenly see blue Porsches everywhere after buying one, or why you notice every pregnant lady in the world once you or your partner are expecting. Your RAS has been programmed to see what matters to your current reality.

The way the TikTok Cat Filter can linger in your perception is the perfect, modern metaphor for how the Reticular Activating System (RAS) works. It's not just noticing something; it's wearing a filter that makes you see only that. The RAS takes the dominant thoughts you feed it—whether positive or negative—and puts a persistent filter over your reality to match them.

If you're constantly thinking about why you can't do something—I'm too old, I don't have time, I'm not a runner—your RAS will dutifully find all the "evidence" to support that limiting belief. It will highlight articles about injuries, point out all the people faster than you, and remind you of every failed attempt. The "I can't filter" is on, and the world looks impossible.

But if you constantly visualize your goals, repeat positive affirmations, and immerse yourself in empowering content, your RAS will start highlighting opportunities, resources, and solutions you never noticed before. Runners unconsciously (and consciously!) train their RAS to spot the path to success, even when their legs are screaming for mercy. They don't just see the finish line; they see the specific spot on the road to focus on, the perfectly-paced runner to draft behind, or the exact moment to take a drink. They are running with the I can filter active, and their RAS is constantly scanning for the next advantage.

When your inner world (Intense Desire) and your actions (Embodied Belief) are in perfect alignment, the outer world naturally reorganizes itself to match your state. The manifestation isn't something you have to chase; it's something that finds you.

The Repetition Supercharger

Now, to truly supercharge this system—to make it a permanent, non-stop magnet—you need one more step: Repetition.

Think of your mind as a hard drive. To install a new, life-changing program (like, I Am A CEO or I Am A Marathon Finisher), you don't just tap the icon once. You have to hit Auto-Repeat until the download is complete, overwriting all that ancient, dusty failure software. Replay the desired object or outcome again and again in your mind. This constant, deliberate firing and wiring is how your RAS takes your thought from a fleeting idea to a permanent, hardwired directive. Repetition is the persistent, loud drumbeat that tells your mind, "Listen up! This is the new reality. We are calling the shots now."

The Subconscious CEO: Stop Running Old Software

Has this ever happened to you? You're determined to change–a behavior, a thought pattern, or a limiting belief, but no matter how hard you push, it never seems to stick. There's a reason, and you're not going to like it: You can crave change all you want, but until you reprogram your subconscious, it simply won't happen.

You've heard the old adage, right? It takes 21–28 days to change a pattern or behavior. That's why successful, sustained efforts like Alcoholics Anonymous require consistent, long-term commitment—they understand the massive effort required to rewire deeply ingrained habits.

Listen up, dove. Here's the truth: You might have a colossal, heart-thumping, mind-blowing vision in your head—that dream life where you're the person you were destined to become. But what if that nagging voice of negativity is still there, whispering doubt in the back of your mind? That's your subconscious, the part of your brain that's been on autopilot for decades. It's like a computer running on a seriously old operating system, complete with bugs, viruses, and a whole lot of outdated programming. And you, my friend, have to become the hacker who installs the new, high-performance software.

The Brain Whisperer

This is where someone like Kelly Howell, a pioneer in subconscious reprogramming comes in. Known as the Brain Whisperer, Howell draws from her own catastrophic car accident in which she broke her neck, which left her suffering from depression and headaches. She knew she had to convince herself to heal, otherwise she might languish and die. That inspired her to explore the power of the mind-body connection and led to the launch of Brain Sync in 1991. Since then, her programs have been used in hospitals, the military, athletic performance and clinics worldwide.

Howell pioneered sound frequencies to gently guide your brain from a busy Beta state into a more relaxed Alpha or Theta state. You're basically bypassing the conscious mind and speaking directly to the subconscious. You're giving it new commands, new beliefs, and new programs to run. It's like installing a brand-new, lightning-fast operating system into your mind. You aren't just telling yourself a new story; you're installing a new truth.

Whatever Your Mind Believes, It Makes Real.

– Kelly Howell

The Subconscious Blueprint: Masters of the Mind

This isn't some woo woo rubbish. The principles of accessing and influencing these deeper states have been used by masters for centuries.

Andrew Carnegie & Napoleon Hill (The Masterminds): Think about Andrew Carnegie, the titan of the steel industry. His mentorship of Napoleon Hill was all about understanding the power of the mind, the "definite major purpose" and persistent visualization – practices that inherently access these deeper, subconscious levels. Hill's entire philosophy in "Think and Grow Rich" is built on the premise that what the mind can conceive and believe, it can achieve, by consciously impressing those desires onto the subconscious.

Nikola Tesla (The Visionary): Tesla used mental rehearsal, running and perfecting complex inventions entirely in his mind for months, effectively debugging his creations on a subconscious level before ever building a prototype.

Thomas Edison (The Sleeper): Edison purposefully accessed the creative, liminal state between wakefulness and sleep. By capturing ideas generated when his conscious mind was "offline," he mined breakthroughs directly from his deeper, uninhibited mind.

These masters, whether in the 1800s or today, understood that true transformation begins within. It's about being an owner of your mental programming, actively shaping the internal script that dictates your actions, your beliefs, and ultimately, your destiny. This isn't magic; it's the disciplined application of universal principles to rewire your most powerful asset: your mind.

So, what are you waiting for, my friend? This isn't just about "thinking positively." It's about stepping into a legacy of titans and pioneers. It's about joining the ranks of the greats who understood that the real game-changer isn't a new app or a bigger bank account; it's the conscious, deliberate, and fiercely disciplined act of owning your mind. This is your birthright. It's time to claim it, rewrite your script, and show the world what a masterpiece looks like.

Visualization: Immersive Futurecasting

We've talked the talk... now lace 'em up: Your Marathon Starts Now! It's one thing to understand the profound power of visualization, and another entirely to put it to work.

It's time to transform the mundane into the magnificent, turning your routine into a training ground for success. Ready to take these powerful principles from the page and electrify your everyday reality? Here are a few scenarios to flex that visualization brawn in your daily lives.

Nailing That Tough Conversation: The Art of Confrontation

The Scenario: You need to have a difficult conversation with a colleague, a client, or even a family member. Your gut tightens, and you start rehearsing all the ways it could go wrong.

The Visualization: Before the actual conversation, find a quiet moment. Close your eyes. See yourself approaching the conversation with calm confidence. Hear yourself articulating your points clearly, assertively, but also empathetically. Feel the positive tension in the room as both parties listen respectfully. Visualize the desired outcome – a resolution, an understanding, a productive next step. See yourself shaking hands, or walking away with a sense of peace.

The Impact: This mental rehearsal programs your brain for success. It reduces anxiety, allows you to anticipate potential sticking points, and mentally prepares you to respond constructively rather than react emotionally. You're not hoping for a good outcome; you're priming yourself for one.

Crushing a Presentation or Job Interview:

The Scenario: You've got a big presentation, a crucial pitch, or a high-stakes job interview looming. The butterflies are flapping with increased intensity.

The Visualization: Go through the entire event in your mind, in vivid detail. See yourself walking into the room, making eye contact, feeling confident and relaxed. Hear your voice delivering your points with clarity and conviction. Feel the energy of the room, the engagement of your audience. Visualize yourself answering tough questions smoothly, perhaps even with a touch of humor. See the positive reactions, the nodding heads, the applause, or the offer being extended.

The Impact: This is pure mental rehearsal. It builds confidence by making the unfamiliar familiar. It reduces performance anxiety because your brain has already "practiced" the successful execution. Your nervous system is primed for the reality you've just visualized.

Improving Relationships:

The Scenario: You're having recurring friction with a specific person, or you want to improve a relationship in general.

The Visualization: Before an interaction, see yourself approaching them with an open mind and a positive attitude. Visualize a harmonious conversation, where you both listen and understand. Feel the warmth of communication, even if it's just a small step forward. And rest assured that you can express your emotions without negative outcomes. It's the art of connecting, not confronting.

The Impact: This prepares you to interact from a place of intention rather than reaction. It helps you project a more positive energy, which often elicits a better response from others. You're setting the stage for a different outcome by changing your internal script first.

Rules of the Road

- You get a Finisher Medal for yanking back your wayward plot
- You discovered the secret to cracking the code: Mental Mastery
- You learned the big reveal: your mind doesn't know the difference between what it imagines and what's real
- You learned to sidestep the icky subway rats of life
- You discovered how to feed the Monitor of Your Mind
- You delved into the beautiful and powerful tools to combat negativity and wire yourself for the win: Visualization, Mental Rehearsal, Subconscious Reprogramming

You flexed your muscles on Visualization Techniques

Bravo.

CHAPTER 9

INVEST IN YOURSELF

People ask me all the time: what was the single best investment of my career?

Was it working at a small but exclusive book club in the late '80s for literary icons like Jason and Barbara Epstein? Was it teaching myself HTML back in the '90s, using that old-school tech Bible from O'Reilly and Sons? Because my Programming buddies at Lehman Brothers insisted I needed to learn "this Internet thing"? Or maybe it was that intensive Data Analytics workshop at NYU, led by Prof Scott Galloway? What about the thrill of getting airtime with the MarTech genius Martin Kihn during the digital Ad explosion?

What single thing contributed to making me the person I am today?

Easy answer. Investing in myself.

Now, don't get me wrong, professional upskilling is absolutely vital. It's the premium, high-octane fuel you pour into your sophisticated engine. You have to learn new techniques, new skills, and new competencies every day. Remember the good old days when getting a Ranger badge in Salesforce was the ultimate flex? When mastering lead tracking in a CRM made you feel like a total boss? Cute. That whole conversation has been totally hijacked by AI, and now everyone's running around like headless chickens scrambling for cutting-edge certifications just to keep up.

But here's the thing: Investing isn't just about the professional upskilling. It's the continuous, radical commitment to your personal evolution. I'm talking about the thousands of hours I've spent devouring the masters of leadership, marketing and personal development. Hundreds of audios—back in the old days, they were on actual cassette tapes! Remember those ancient relics? I poured time and cash into workshops, webinars, podcasts, videos, tutorials, and classes. For one single purpose: To step into my own greatness and build a life I was wildly in love with.

The Chemistry Set: Investing in Biology

I treat my body like a high-end, highly temperamental chemistry set. I'm constantly testing, titrating, and micro-dosing to keep my entire system in harmonic balance. That means investing in all my magnificent systems—musculoskeletal, immune, endocrine, hormonal, vascular—to keep them humming and optimized.

I pop my supplements like they're Tictacs. Tinctures, inhalers, sublingual drops (under the tongue) to maximize absorption and get the biggest, quickest hit to my entire being. It takes time. And commitment to my schedule, my body, and yes, my wallet!

But boy does it pay off. We're talking next-level bio-hacking that makes Geritol look like a carrier pigeon sending a group text–all heart, but no bandwidth. I make it my mission to research and ingest the cutting-edge discoveries by specialists like Dr. David Sinclair, the foremost authority on Anti-Aging. This Harvard luminary has spent decades developing a serum to reverse aging. Imagine hitting 100 years, without disease, without ruined hips and knees, or failing organs and systems. Hello, future self! This isn't science fiction; this is science in action.

Then there's the mushroom maestro, Paul Stamets, the super cool author of "Mycelium Running: How Mushrooms Can Help Save the World". If you're hitting those inevitable "senior moments"—where did I put my keys? Why did I walk into the garage?–his products for mental acuity are freaking awesome! But here's the real kicker: Stamets' groundbreaking research goes way beyond just finding your keys. We're talking about fungi as the ultimate internal neuro-allies for memory, immunity and athletic recovery.

The longevity craze isn't just for athletes. Tech titans like Jeff Bezos, Larry Ellison, and Sam Altman are sinking fortunes into bio-optimization. Even Elon Musk is investing in his health—because you have to be in shape to conquer Mars.

Every single system–your cellular energy engines, DNA's control settings, hormonal cascade, neuroplasticity, immunity, and cellular renewal—has the potential for radical improvement. Delaying decay is now purely a matter of choice, not chance. Which is great news for that magnificent body of yours.

The Investment = Never Stagnating

But wait, there's one more mind-blowing piece of the puzzle. This relentless investment means the absolute opposite of stagnation. It's permission to do stuff you've never dared before. It means embracing the wild willingness to step into the shoes of the person you have yet to become.

So, how do you actually pull that off? How do you burn the bridge behind you, shed the skin of the "safe" person you were yesterday, and embrace the glorious, scary unknown that's not even a flicker of a dream?

You need a disruptor. You need a spectacular agent of chaos. You need a guide who actively seeks out newness and will force you to get uncomfortable. You need proof that what you haven't yet dared to dream is absolutely possible. You just need the knowledge to write the new code.

Unlocking the Future: Why Your Yesterday Can't See Tomorrow

Everybody needs a friend like Michele. She is the Genie of gift-giving. For some uncanny reason, she just intuitively knows a person's deepest desire and then figures out a way to make it happen.

Case in point: for her triathlete husband's 50th birthday, she gave him a trip to France with his buddies to follow the Tour de France, ride the same legendary roads as the cyclists, and finish up in Paris at the race finale! They had VIP passes to hang out with the pros, watch them warm up, and even drink champagne with the official Tour de France logo. You can imagine how he devoured that gift like the champion of the mountains! He never would have even dreamed an adventure like that for himself.

But Michele did.

She dreams up new experiences and creates the best presents ever, and you know why? Because Michele is literally wired for expansion. She doesn't crave comfort; she craves the discomfort of the unknown—new tastes, new sounds, new skills, new adventures. She treats every sunrise like an invitation to explore a territory she's never mapped before. Her philosophy isn't just a simple saying; it's a battle cry against stagnation: "If I don't try something new every day, I feel like I miss out on the day."

And that my friends, is the kicker. Because if you're not careful, your history is limiting your future. You literally can't dream beyond what your past has already served up to you. How could you? That's why you have to get outside of your own limitations. And the only way to do that? Stop thinking like yourself.

The Alter-Ego Protocol: The Framework for Your Future Self

Ready to actively interrupt your habitual thought patterns and push past your "discomfort" territory? The Alter-Ego Protocol is a temporary, radical identity shift designed to obliterate your limitations and unlock solutions you didn't know existed. Think of this as stepping into the shoes of your Future Self—the one who already has the success, the confidence, and the answers.

Your Mission: From Stagnation into Your Future Self

Forget the long game. This is a powerful, focused 24-hour test designed to shock your brain out of stagnation and tap into your future self.

Step 1–Create Your Champion: Define the person who is not constrained by your history

- Name It: Give this power identity a name that instantly evokes the trait you want to borrow like: The Fearless Negotiator, The Sovereign Strategist, The Decisive Architect, The Unshakeable Empress.

- Set the Rule: Choose one non-negotiable core belief that is the absolute opposite of your current limiting tendency. If you tend to overthink: Make decisions in under 5 seconds. If you tend to avoid confrontation: State the hardest truth clearly and immediately.

- Adopt the Stance: How does this person physically carry themselves? Choose a distinct posture, walking pace, and vocal tone. This is the physical trigger you will use to step into the role. *Example: Standing tall, shoulders back, and speaking in a slower, deeper register. Making eye contact fearlessly.*

- Identify Three High-Leverage Decisions: Locate three points during the upcoming day where you usually revert to a safe, historical decision (e.g., choosing lunch, approaching a difficult email, or starting/abandoning a task). The Alter-Ego must handle these three points.

Step 2 – Execute the Shock: For one full day, your "normal self" is on vacation

Commit fully to the persona for one full day. Your goal is to experience the world through their unrestricted perspective.

- The Trigger: As soon as you wake up, mentally announce the Unshakeable Empress, or the name you chose, and adopt their Power Stance. Remember, your "normal self" is on vacation for the next 24 hours.

- Challenge Your History: For every decision, large or small, ask yourself: "How would [Alter-Ego Name] handle this, ignoring what I usually do?"
  - If the Alter-Ego would choose the 5 a.m. run, you run.
  - If the Alter-Ego would pitch an ambitious idea, you pitch it.
  - If the Alter-Ego would ask the interesting guy at Panera out, you ask him out.

- Embrace the Alien: The most effective moments of the day will be the ones that feel awkward or unnatural. That feeling of discomfort is proof that you are successfully breaking a deeply ingrained behavioral pattern. Welcome it.

- Journal in Character: At lunchtime or a quiet moment, write a paragraph describing the day so far, using the Alter-Ego's vocabulary and voice. This deepens the immersion and committing to paper ingrains a mental, visual and emotional pact.

Step 3–The 1% Pledge: Integrate Your Future Self

You've officially tapped into the vein of your Future Self–the one who doesn't wait for permission. Now it's time to incorporate that gold into your daily life.

- The Shocking Results: Review your journal entries or simply recall the day. Answer these two critical questions:
    1. Find the Breakthrough: Review the day and identify the outcome(s) your normal self would have deemed impossible or too risky? What did the Champion achieve?
    2. What feeling (e.g., relief, confidence, lightness) was associated with making the high-leverage decisions differently?

- The 1% Pledge: Identify one habit, phrase, or rule—that you will permanently integrate into your "normal" life.
    1. Example: You adopt the Alter-Ego's habit of immediately clearing your desk before leaving work.
    2. Example: You adopt the Alter-Ego's ability to say the things you really want to say without fear or anger.

Step 4: The Future Dream

Based on the new perspective gained during your Alter-Ego Day, write down one future goal you previously limited yourself from pursuing. This new goal is your first step in Unlocking the Future.

Living Your Best Life

Everyone's talking about it. But what if the "best life" everyone talks about isn't even on your radar? What if you've been told to live your best life, but the only life you can see right now is a dismal, grim existence based on old, tired programming and potentially lies?

That's why your past is limiting your future. Kiss your old self sayonara. Thanks for all the memories. I'm ready for a new upgrade, and it's gonna be epic. Because you're not just learning new skills but becoming a different person. A brand new, more aware, and yup, I'm going to say it—a more *selfish* person.

| Self Help – Because If You Don't Help Yourself, Who Will?

MROY – Maximize the Return on You

Tell me the truth. You give a lot to the people you love right? You hunt down the latest Louis for your wife. You snag season tickets for your man. Your kids make out like bandits at Christmas. Your pet's food, treats and meds are all on auto-refill with Chewy.

You give a lot to others! So when does that compass turnaround and target you? When do you make yourself the target of all that devotion and support?

The answer is now. The practice of self-help is simply the conscious decision to put your own growth first. We call this commitment to relentless effort the Maximize the Return on You (MROY) principle. MROY means treating your own potential as the most valuable asset you possess, pouring all your resources—time, dedication, and effort—into becoming the person who can achieve anything.

When you invest this deeply in yourself, the returns are often profound, public, and legendary. Let's look at ways to maximize the investment in you, and a few folks who have heavily MROY-ed with dramatic results.

10 Habits to MROY

1. Unpack Your Authentic Code

Learn one high-value skill that 99% of people lack, Narrative Crafting, AI Prompt Engineering, Elite Negotiation or Complex Deal Structuring. Your financial value equals your unique knowledge. Become the connoisseur of your own authenticity.

The ultimate MVP of this strategy is Mr. Beast—Jimmy Donaldson. This social media titan proved that being your authentic self can equal uber success. His superpower is radical generosity wrapped in a prank. He's not just an influencer; he's a departure model. He took his unique, sometimes capricious gifts, embraced them, and built a global philanthropic empire. He uses the massive wealth from his challenges to fund even bigger ones—a flawless, self-sustaining loop. Your unique skill should do the same for you.

2. Buy Compressed Wisdom

Let's talk pure MROY: You don't have time for the full 10,000-hour slog. Your solution? Buy someone else's insight. Book the expert, snag the mentor, or hire the coach. Look at Kelly Lynn Adams, a top-tier Business and Life Coach. She embodies the spectacular agent of chaos you need. She doesn't just offer suggestions; she acts as the disruptor who steps in to fundamentally interrupt the old, failing program, forcing an immediate, exponential shift in your Identity, Income, and Impact.

Her service is the transfer of a highly successful "codebase" directly into your life, dramatically shortening your learning curve and leapfrogging years ahead. This move is not a luxury; it's the necessary hack that all high achievers, leaders, and even other Coaches use! Borrow another's wisdom, download their code, and make their brilliance your own.

3. Empower Your Personal Infrastructure: Eliminate the Drag

Your day is already a high-stakes marathon. Why let constant friction— the squeaky chair, the buffering Wi-Fi, the endless small decisions suck the precious energy right out of you? Your third MROY investment is in Superlative Infrastructure. This means proactively eliminating the drag on your daily life, turning energy drains into energy boosts. Hunt down the ergonomic chair that makes you feel weightless. Automate your finances to free up mental space.

Take back your time, like when I bought a set of BOSE noise-canceling headphones for my brutal two-hour daily commute. Instead of listening to other people chatter about their shore houses, I plugged in and filled my head with beautiful, restorative sounds. I used that previously lost time to fuel my mind with Chopin's Etudes, the gentle sound of ocean waves to catch some shut eye, or guided meditations from Joe Dispenza or Vaz Sriharan to change my frequency. When you flip an energy drag into a focused, personal benefit, the MROY is truly immeasurable. This is how you optimize your environment for victory.

4. From Finish Lines to Chief Running Officer

Bart Yasso MROYed by doing something completely counterintuitive: He turned his running shoes into his highest-yielding investment fund. His initial "investment" wasn't just time or effort; it was a relentless, almost singular devotion to the sport. He poured every resource into his potential—not just running major marathons on earth, but also showing up for every runner, everywhere. The MROY for Bart wasn't just physical health; the returns unlocked unprecedented professional ascent and unparalleled influence. He became the Chief Running Officer for Runner's World, established the globally recognized Yasso 800s training plan, and built a legacy as "the Mayor of Running." Bart is particularly proud of two distinctions: Being inducted into the Running USA Hall of Champions and the Road Runners Club of America Distance Running Hall of Fame. He proved when you invest completely in your purpose, the dividend is a life of legendary influence.

5. Architect Your Mastermind Alliance

You are the average of the five people you spend the most time with, said the incomparable Jim Rhone. To achieve 10x the results, you must actively seek out people who are already operating at a level 10x beyond YOU. As Porter Gale's book says, "Your network is your net worth." You cannot climb a mountain alone. You need a team of high-altitude climbers to lift you to the summit.

The ultimate blueprint for this comes straight from the mind of Andrew Carnegie, who formalized the power of the Mastermind Group:

- The Strategic Five: Strategically surround yourself with a compact group of highly specialized champions whose skills are complementary, not redundant, to your own. You don't need yes-men; you need assassins of inefficiency and exponential thinkers.

- Zero-Ego Alignment: Cultivate a genuine atmosphere of mutual respect where all ideas are exchanged freely, and failure is a shared learning tool. This non-competitive alignment is the fuel for collective breakthroughs.

- The Defined Major Purpose: The entire purpose of this collective energy must be laser-focused on attaining a turbo-charged goal. The Mastermind is a vehicle for acceleration, not just conversation.

Here's a Purpose my Mastermind Group chases: *Establish members of this collective as nationally recognized, undisputed thought leaders in their respective fields.*

6. Forge Mental Armor

High ambition is a contact sport, and chaos is the opponent. You need emotional resilience—or you'll get knocked out. Let's talk about the ultimate stockholder when it comes to the self investment: David Goggins. This man isn't just an extreme athlete; he's a human case study in MROY taken to the absolute, unforgiving limit. Goggins's biggest investment wasn't in gear or trainers; it was in becoming the unshakeable master of his own mind. He famously crushed the "inner whiner" by silencing the pathetic chatter and pushing past the physical agony that screams quit. That commitment to relentlessly pushing the perceived limit is the purest, rawest form of investing in your mental capacity. This is what it means to Invest Hard.

7. Master Delay: Time is Your Horizon

Before it was a glorious, 1.28-mile-long ribbon of steel, open to hikers and cyclists, offering mind-blowing views of the Hudson Valley, it was just the Poughkeepsie-Highland Railroad Bridge. It burned down in 1974 and was left derelict for thirty years, a massive, rusting skeleton of forgotten potential. Then came Fred Schaeffer. He didn't see junk; he saw legacy. He saw a public park, a new center for community, and infrastructure that would change the economy of the Hudson Valley. This wasn't a quick fix; it was a vision that required grit, patience, and the relentless, non-negotiable belief that the long-term payoff was worth the decades of struggle. Fred fought bureaucracy, rallied a community, secured funding, and transformed that abandoned 19th century steel into a 21st century marvel. This monumental project, which took years of his life and dedication to realize, is the definition of a long-haul commitment.

The lesson? Stop chasing instant gratification. If your goal doesn't feel slightly insane to the average person right now, it's probably not big enough. See the potential, ignore the rust.

8. Refill Your Cup

Running at a high level is unsustainable without a ruthless recovery strategy. Meet Chinazom Sunny Nwabueze, a High Stakes Decisions Strategist who coaches C-Suite leaders through crisis and chaos. He's also an accomplished athlete who knows how to navigate personal tempests.

Chinazom hit his ultimate Wall during a brutal duathlon—a moment where the pain stops being physical and starts screaming at your mind. He calls them the "demons," the loud voice that tells you "absolutely untruths" to make you quit. Every ambitious human eventually faces this deceitful foe.

His magical, MROY strategy? He laughs at negativity. This isn't about ignoring the pain; it's about reframing it. Chinazom has learned to invest in himself – as an athlete, a father, a husband, and a business owner – by making sure he refills his cup. He consciously identifies what needs to go into that cup: what brings him joy, what restores him, what allows him to simply be. As an entrepreneur and leader, you must invest in yourself by consciously identifying what fills your cup. Rest, Recovery, and Rejuvenation isn't a luxury item you can skip. It is the ultimate MROY strategy. If you don't make space for it, you cannot possibly show up fully and conquer your next adventure.

9. Conquer the Unknown

You cannot maximize your return if you play within known limits. MROY demands you intentionally venture into the terrifying unknown. In 2024, Jasmin Paris did the impossible, becoming the first woman in history to finish the infamous Barkley Marathons—arguably the hardest race on the planet. Race director, Lazarus Lake literally declared the race "too hard for women." Jasmin took him up on the challenge–two attempts, and one ultimate mic drop.

This isn't your weekend jog, people. Barkley is a legendary, 60-hour ultrarun with an elevation gain equivalent to summiting Mount Everest *twice*. The rules are pure, glorious insanity: no GPS, just a map, a compass, and pages ripped from books hidden in the woods as proof. If you quit, a bugle plays Taps. James Earl Ray, Martin Luther King's assassin, only made it eight miserable miles before being caught–that's how brutal this course is.

Jasmin's historic finish was the ultimate payoff on her MROY. She's a full-time veterinarian and a mother of two–she didn't have time for failure. Only 20 individuals have ever finished this race since 1986, and Jasmin is the only woman. Her success wasn't just for her; it was a testament to radical self-investment, fueled by the desire to conquer the unknown. She handed a massive dose of inspiration to "women worldwide... to believe in themselves."

10. Prioritization is Transferrable

If the goal of MROY is the optimal allocation of finite time, energy, and focus across a complex life, then John Kelly is the ultimate Master of the Pacing Plan. He's finished the soul-crushing Barkley Marathons THREE times and this year attempted a personal best time on the Appalachian Trail—all while being a committed family man and a renowned tech co-founder. He proves you don't have to sacrifice one pillar of life to succeed in another.

Kelly's life is a constant, high-stakes negotiation where most leaders would crumble. He demonstrates radical ownership over three key elements: "Careful Prioritization, Scheduling, and Communication". It was a massive learning process to trim out the excess and focus only on what truly matters. Here's the power move: His secret sauce is integration. His wife, family, job, and running are fully aware of what's going on in the other areas. They communicate it, schedule it, and make it work. His family is often his support crew, which allows him to integrate his passions rather than create separation.

He looks at his life like a "constrained optimization problem". It's not about magically finding extra time; it's about asking: What is the absolute maximum I can achieve with the resources and constraints I have right now? Kelly strips away the myth of superhuman achievement, showing us that any epic feat is the product of relentless focus and absolute prioritization.

The Strive Economy: The Lie of Control

Control is a beautiful thing, until we realize we have none of it. You spend your life grinding in the Strive Economy—hustling, micromanaging every tiny detail like a hyper-caffeinated chess champion, convinced that if you just work hard enough, the Universe will cough up your prize.

Guess what? Winning is ephemeral. You see it all the time with elite athletes: One minute they're crushing it, and then the next, they look like they just ate a Kale McMuffin. How do the pros reset? They ditch the frantic striving and come back to a place of fierce acceptance. They drop the how and focus on the why. They say: My goal is pure. My intent is here. I love this game.

The Micro-Management Trap

I get it. I'm a list maker, too. My friends call me the Post-it Queen. Lists are great for organizing your tasks, but they are not your security blanket!

We push too hard, strategizing every single micro-move. That's not being prepared; that's the **Micro-Management Trap**, and it's the fastest way to kill your vibe:

- The Backpack of BS: You're constantly hauling around a heavy backpack of self-imposed pressure, checking off cans of metaphorical soup you don't even need to carry. Ditch the damn pack!

- The CPU Drain: Your brain is running a 24/7 internal scroll, searching for the one thing you missed. Stop wasting your bandwidth on imaginary problems!

- The Rewind Habit: You replay conversations and decisions because you can't trust your own judgment. Newsflash: You're amazing. Stop checking your work!

- Pre-Emptive Anxiety: You're spoiling the gorgeous present moment by freaking out over a future that hasn't even loaded yet. Cut. It. Out.

- The Google Calendar Gridlock: The Universe dares to make your meeting run three minutes overtime, and you immediately feel a full-body panic because your entire, meticulously planned day is now "off schedule." Flexibility is wealth, darling. Stop monetizing your minutes!

- The External Validation Loop: Needing immediate, glowing feedback on every tiny decision you make (did I send that email right? was that meeting joke funny?) instead of trusting your own stellar instincts. Your mirror is the only judge that matters.

Auto Pilot

Now Auto Pilot—that's different. Auto Pilot means you've done the programming and the testing. Now it runs on its own. The investment isn't in control; it's in trust. You can let go and trust that you've done the work, allowing you to enjoy the fruits of your labor without having to orchestrate the perfect day.

| Far Niente – The Art of Doing Nothing

A few years ago we visited a fabulously gorgeous vineyard called Far Niente. While every inch of the vineyard and tasting room was lush and beautiful, the name itself still curls my toes.

The Italians have mastered this concept of allowing Auto Pilot to take over. They call it Il Dolce Far Niente—the sweetness of doing nothing. It's an art form, a conscious, joyful abandonment of productivity. It's accepting that the most valuable thing you can do right now is simply *be*. It's the ultimate counter-program to the Strive Economy.

The Messy Backslide is Your Upgrade Notification

Listen: You broke up with your old self when you decided to elevate. That former you is now throwing a rebellion, confusing your emotions and making you backslide. That's just your emotional body shedding the old vibration. You were doing so good! And you still are!

When you choose a new pattern, it's never seamless. It's messy. It's hard. You'll want to crawl back into your comfort zone, even if that zone feels like a scratchy, ill-fitting burlap sack that makes you sneeze.

Embrace the Gimp: Why Your New Pattern Might Start Ugly

Let me tell you a secret about building new patterns. When I was 10, I decided to teach myself to write left-handed, all because I read in Teen Beat magazine that a pop star broke his arm (don't ask). I'd scribble these wild escapades about a fictitious dude named Joe Captain, who was a bit of a dimwit but faced adventures that blew my juvenile mind.

My penmanship was ghastly. Letters slanted everywhere. It was barely legible. But I knew I had to carve a new pattern, just in case my right arm became Mr. Gimp. I had epics to write, you know? So I laughed it off. I still revisit those scribbles for a chuckle—and to give myself credit. Changing isn't easy. When you kick off a new behavior, a new pattern, it's never brilliant. It's hard. And you will always want to go back to your comfort zone, even if that zone doesn't honor the optimized person you're becoming.

> *"There is nothing noble in being superior to your fellow man; true nobility is being superior to your former self."*
>
> *– Ernest Hemingway*

Give yourself credit, laugh at the mistakes, and keep showing up. The ultimate secret to the long game is patience. That feeling of hitting a wall—that plateau—is simply a necessary period where your mind and body are consolidating gains before your next major breakthrough. You are not failing; you are LEVELING UP.

Learn to Love and Trust the Plateau

You got addicted to the thrill of self-victory, right? The initial surge is amazing—the rapid, exciting gains! But guess what? That high fades, the improvements slow down, and BAM! You hit the dreaded Plateau.

This is where almost everyone quits. They look at the leveling off and mistake it for failure. They think they've lost their edge. But this messy, frustrating feeling is what the long game is all about. This is Your Hardware Upgrade, kiddo.

The plateau is NOT a failure state. It's your System Integration Period. Your body and mind are demanding this downtime because they're busy cementing all those insane gains you just made! Think of it as hardening the infrastructure so you don't break down on the way to the next peak.

For Your Body: It's the essential muscle recovery and adaptation. You know you can't crush a heavy lift every single day. Rest isn't laziness; it's the required time to rebuild stronger and more powerful than before.

For Your Brain: This is the cool part: it's Myelination time. Your brain is literally insulating the neural highways you just spent weeks creating. It takes those frantic, conscious struggles and makes them automatic—moving you from thinking about every step to becoming unconsciously competent. You're building an Auto-Pilot that actually works.

This messy, backsliding feeling is what the long game is all about. When you talk about MROY, your instinct is to chase exponential growth—a new peak every month. True return isn't measured in short sprints; it's measured in decades of elevated performance.

Lessons from Boston

Amby Burfoot, the Boston Marathon champion, knew the secret. He said the frustration of hitting a wall is often a sign of impending change, not failure. His philosophy is pure gold: "We runners simply don't get better fast enough to satisfy ourselves... We should be more tortoise-like. For that is the path to success… Give yourself time. Don't make hasty and unnecessary mistakes. Remember: You're in it for the long run. Life is a marathon, not a sprint; pace yourself accordingly."

In essence, patience is the critical skill you're missing when you feel stuck. The plateau isn't a dead end, it's a necessary period where your mind and body are consolidating gains before the next breakthrough.

Remember the 15th-century poet Rumi? He advised couples to "let there be spaces in your togetherness." You need those spaces! You can't live at the peak all the time. There must be Gaps in Your Peaks. That silence, that level ground—that's your foundation getting rock solid for the next big leap.

The Dreaded Dopamine Descent

That deep, unadulterated pleasure of winning should last forever, right? But the tension between that peak moment of victory and the quiet flatness that can follow is real. It's the reason many people find themselves battling a post-peak slump just when they should be celebrating.

I want to share something vital I heard on the Huberman Lab podcast recently. It's a game-changer for understanding that post-peak slump! We all know good old dopamine, right? It's the naturally produced neurotransmitter—the one that drives movement, mood, and, most importantly, REWARD. It's that lovely, euphoric feeling when you achieve something... but let's be realistic, it's also a highly effective, naturally occurring drug.

Here's the kicker, though: After that massive dopamine jolt, it doesn't just settle back down to normal. Oh no. It drops to a level LOWER than where it started. Think about it! Our everyday hits? Caffeine and chocolate. But you get this hit from even secondary experiences—like watching a screen!

Check this out: You're watching Gordon Ramsay chew through a terrifying spicy wing on **The Hot Ones**. You're cracking up at his profanity. You're pumped, you're hysterical, you're swimming in dopamine! But then the video ends. The laughter fades and the spice subsides. And suddenly? That dopamine level plunges, leaving you feeling strangely confused, flat, or just... sad.

Stop Feeding the Gremlins: Seek Balance

To understand exactly why this plunge happens, it's time to talk neuroscience, courtesy of Dr. Anna Lembke, Chief of Addiction Science at Stanford. In her book, *Dopamine Nation*, she uses the metaphor of a Pleasure Pain Balance—think of it as a mental teeter-totter. When you get that massive dopamine jolt (the euphoric high from a victory, a huge rush of sugar, or endless scrolling), the balance tips hard to the side of pleasure. But your brain is obsessed with getting back to level, which neuroscientists call homeostasis.

The catch? Your brain overshoots. Lembke calls the self-regulating mechanisms that bring you back down the little 'neuro-adaptation gremlins'—and they don't hop off when the balance is level. They stay on the pain side until the teeter-totter is tipped an equal and opposite amount into deficit.

That's the secret behind the post-peak slump! You were swimming in dopamine, and now your level plunges lower than where it started. You feel flat, anxious, and craving something—anything—just to feel normal again. This constant chasing leads to tolerance, meaning you need more and more of the same behavior just to get a smaller and smaller effect.

The fix? A simple, radical act: Abstain completely for four weeks. Instead of trying to find the next jolt, the next social IV drip—just sit. Sit with the craving, the anxiety and yes—the deep, miserable BOREDOM! But after those hard weeks? The magic happens: your baseline resets. Suddenly, simple, organic pleasures—like genuine connection over coffee or the taste of a quiet meal—return. This is the way of the Marathon Mindset – retraining your mind and emotions to finally be at ease. You'll know deep down that you are meant to be fully present in this human body, savoring the simple act of being yourself.

When We Had to Look People in the Eyes

You're probably thinking, "Surviving a meeting without glancing at my phone is a hostage negotiation." But trust me, I'm about to tell you something that sounds like it belongs in an archaeological textbook, even though it was less than two decades ago: The iPhone didn't even exist until 2007.

Think about that! A world where kids, parents, celebrities, and even politicians weren't permanently glued to a glowing, infinitely distracting rectangle. What did we do? We were forced to engage in activities now considered extreme sports:

- We had actual conversations over coffee, looking directly into the other person's eyes—a truly terrifying prospect.

- We suffered through the silence of a queue, relying on our own thoughts or, worse, having to read the ingredients list on the back of a shampoo bottle for entertainment.

- We watched the world outside the car window, instead of passively consuming the endless scroll feed.

This isn't ancient history; it's just the history of non-distraction. We were forced to deal with the real, unbuffered world, and here's the secret: we survived. We can still unclip that digital leash and reconnect with the wonderfully awkward, demanding, and ultimately richer reality waiting for us.

The Goal is Icing, The Journey is Cake

The message is humble, but utterly profound: Enjoy Your Journey. Stop trying to fill every moment with your next rush. Relish where you are, who you are now. Sure, you can fight for a tidy, less convoluted expedition. Or you can sit back and accept the adventure, the humor, and the beautiful mess of that journey.

Guess what my cupcake, your triumphant, finisher goal is the buttercream icing whipped up by Mary Berry. The sponge cake you measured, stirred and baked is the real journey—the real treat, the real fairytale.

How many ways can I say this? Let's try a few, because I want to save you months, maybe years! of torment. Enjoy the Journey!

7 WAYS TO ENJOY THE JOURNEY

1   Guzzle the Grand Tour

2	**Savor the Unscripted**
3	**Find Peace in the Process**
4	**Let Yourself be Guided**
5	**Trust the Detour**
6	**Glide Through the Ride**
7	**The Path is the Heaven**

Human-KIND

This entire discussion—from the science of the dopamine dip to the philosophy of the journey—leads us to one vital, overarching conclusion about how we engage with the world and each other.

Think about our name as a species: Human-Kind. Not Human-Greedy. Not Human-Bigot. We are the only species on earth capable of capturing history, writing symphonies, and peering into the fabric of the universe. We have this elevated status as Masters of the Universe in our own minds, yet our day-to-day existence is often defined by the absolute lowest forms of interaction. Why do we spend so much energy attacking, alienating, and criticizing each other? Why the constant rush toward division, conflict, and judgment?

The Three Sneaky Sources of Negativity

Negativity doesn't just happen; it's an engineered problem. Before you can master your internal world, you have to recognize the three primary channels through which this poisonous voice gains access to your operating system:

- The Ancient Default: The inherited survival programming of our ancestral and internal wiring that treats social exclusion and change as physical pain (The Tribe).
- The Consensus Trap: The pressure of societal and tribal expectations that demands conformity, convincing you that your potential is limited by their definition of "normal."
- The External Bombardment: The intentional bombardment from social media and news, creating a pervasive feeling of despair from manufactured crises, like the threat of AI, to hold your attention.

The Blame Game: Rejecting Partition

These destructive forces—the endless noise, the pressure to perform, the lack of intentionality—all combine to push you toward the laziest, easiest choice there is: Externalization. We constantly fall back on one easy target: The Other Guy.

News feeds and social media haven't just encouraged this tendency; they've weaponized it, creating a massive, profit-driven cycle of blame. We seek endless distraction, quick amusement, and a quiet jolt of voyeurism from strangers because it's easier than looking inward. When in truth, you are simply investing your precious focus in the success of other people who have one ultimate goal: to hijack your focus and turn your clicks into cash.

This constant outward focus fuels the age-old, devious agenda of partition and blame. As a consumer, you are literally paying for this division with your attention and your emotional energy. It's an insane transaction.

My advice? Don't Buy It! Stop letting other people and algorithms profit from your anger and distraction. Reclaim your focus and your power by choosing internal clarity over external chaos.

Other People's Crap Isn't Your Problem

Look, I'm the first to admit I get triggered. When some entitled twit steals my parking spot or a passive-aggressive email makes my blood boil, I'm ready for a nuclear meltdown.

But here is the Truthbomb for your rage: Every single conflict, frustration, and sense of injustice you feel stems from a single, quiet realization: Someone has done or said something that *You Would Not.* Think of it as the ultimate 'You Do You' admission, where you simply step back and watch the internal drama fade away. This isn't weak inspiration; it's rocket science for your inner peace.

Your red-hot fury is purely the result of holding up a mirror and judging another's behavior against your own high-vibrational, personal standards. They failed your test. The moment you acknowledge this truth—"That is something I would never do, and that is why I am losing my mind"—you step straight out of the fight and into independence.

Why? Because their behavior is not a personal attack; it is simply a sad, tired reflection of their default operating system. It has nothing to do with you.

> *"Contrast is the Killer of Joy"–Frank Skuthan, Banking Exec & Marathoner*

The minute you realize this, you've won. You don't have to fix them or fight them, you get to reclaim all that wasted emotional energy. Take a breath, thank the Universe for your clarity, and get back to enjoying your own fabulous run.

Spotted Lantern Fly Badge

Gaps in your peaks are normal; they rejuvenate you for your next climb. Neutral judgment is the kindest gift you can give yourself and others. The slippery slide back to your default setting is inevitable. And yes, you will hear the dragon roar negative things at you every so often. Relax, the IRS isn't lurking around the corner for your MROY receipts! This whole journey should feel like a privilege, not a punishment. And instead of sitting subserviently by, take control and squash out those thoughts.

Our teenage friend Hailey is an accomplished artist that reveres nature. She paints it, sculpts it and defends it. She even has a dance to protect nature from a pesky little bug that's been making waves. I know you've seen them. Those pretty but wretched Spotted Lantern Flies that wreak havoc on trees and shrubs. Hailey created her own dance to squash those beasties. She stomps on the bug, then does a little ballerina pirouette, to make sure it's dead. Because they are sneaky little bastards, and evade approaching footsteps like a ninja.

So. Do your Lantern Fly Dance. Stomp out the flies of mistrust and backslide. Crush those pesky thoughts that plague you. Maybe you bust out the Jitterbug to shake off frantic, anxious energy, or use a powerful Flamenco stamp to ground yourself with pure rhythmic commitment. Perhaps you wriggle a twerk to crush chaotic flareups in your day. Or a smooth, calculated Waltz to bring balance while you struggle with The Plateau. And now, every time you stomp out the insect of negativity, give yourself a Spotted Lantern Fly Badge.

Give Yourself a Badge – You've Earned It!

The true MROY payoff isn't just finishing the race; it's the tiny, powerful mental victory you win every single day. Award yourself a Spotted Lantern Fly Badge for crushing the pests of doubt, avoidance, and fear.

Spotted Lantern Fly Badge

**Every time you stomp out the Insect of Negativity
GIVE YOURSELF A BADGE**

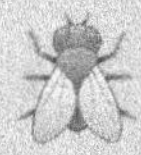

You finish your scheduled workout, not because you set a new personal record, but simply because you honored your commitment to consistency.

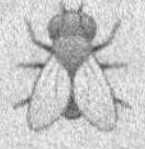

It's your Story. It's Your Glory.

You've successfully built the foundation, invested in your systems, and felt the sweet seduction of dopamine. That's the power of Maximize the Return on You (MROY) in action. With your cup full and your Spotted Lantern Fly stomping game strong, you're not just ready for the next adventure— you're ready to launch it. And every hard-won step on the Plateau is wiring you for permanent glory.

Rules of the Road

- You get a Finisher Medal for investigating how to Invest in Yourself

- You discovered how your History Could be Limiting your Future

- You met heroes who showcase the 10 Keys to MROY–Maximize Return on You

- You paused yourself for 24 hours to discover The Framework for Your Future Self

- You learned to avoid the Micro-Management Trap

- You delved into the beautiful art of Far Niente

- You summited a surprise: The Plateau is your Friend

- You earned Spotted Lantern Fly Badge for stomping out the insects of mistrust

Ready to celebrate your victory? Turn the page.

CHAPTER 10

READY FOR YOUR VICTORY LAP?

My husband, Wayne Gibbons, is an ultra-runner who has been challenging his limits for 5 decades. His personal stats are staggering: more than 350 marathons and 120 ultra-marathons. These are the soul-crushing, 48-hour death marches that make your treadmill look like nap time. His lifetime odometer clocks his mileage around 125,000 miles; that's 225 million steps taken purely in the name of physical and mental investment. For half a century, his body was a machine, driven by unyielding motion.

But the machine ran into a challenge it couldn't outrun.

First, the pandemic. As a practicing chiropractor and acupuncturist, his hands-on business was shut down—no hands meant no treatments, and no patients. For 10 long months, the man who had only known perpetual motion discovered the sweet relief of a forced stop. When businesses reopened, he jumped back in at just three days a week, declaring it his semi-retirement. He liked it.

The ultimate twist arrived in 2024, compliments of a mandatory knee replacement. Get this–the road didn't do him in, a car did! After running every single day—the machine was finally told to stand down. The surprising truth? He was relieved. He had run the race; he won the damn trophy.

The takeaway is simple, profound, and REQUIRED READING for your soul: When you've busted your butt and built your empire—when you've crossed your personal finish line—you stop fighting and you start feasting.

You earned the right to ditch the accumulation hustle and step straight into pure reward.

Wayne calls this new phase of his life exactly what it is: The Victory Lap. It's when you realize the real payoff isn't the medal; it's the sheer, unadulterated pleasure of seeing how far your own two feet carried you.

"We get sick when we don't live our potential" – *George Sheehan*

The Journey Recapped

When we started this journey, the goal was to unearth the culprits that led to perpetual negativity. We discovered that your mind is often held captive by unseen forces designed to keep you small. Through these pages you have discovered:

The Anatomy of the Trap:

Wired for Negativity: Your emotional brain defaults to negativity as an ancient survival mechanism—it's the comfort zone of your inherited genetic story and tribal beliefs.

The Dopamine Drop: The biological reason for the "post-peak slump"— the dreaded Dopamine Descent where your brain overshoots balance, which plunges you into a deficit, leaving you flat and anxious.

External Attack: You are being intentionally targeted and played by the external forces of Social Media, News and global developments. They pose as entertainment, but their sole intent is keeping you engaged, enraged and hopeless.

The Energetic Static: You are constantly swimming in an invisible sea of electronic static—the silent, high-frequency onslaught from Wi-Fi, cell towers, digital waves, and constant device transmissions that contribute to nervous system overload and emotional fatigue.

The Final Leg: Reclaiming Your Medal

The good news is that the game is now over. You've uncovered the Anatomy of the Trap. You know how the ancient programming, the chemical imbalances, the external targeting, and the energetic static work together to keep you small and stressed. You are no longer an unwitting participant. And you know how to claim your triumph by the techniques I shared in these pages.

The Path to the Finish Line:

- Have you given the movie of your life a review? Have you given it the Roger Ebert plot study and asked if it's living up to your dream script? If not, write a new one.

- Which of the Architects of Anxiety will you demolish or refuse to take orders from? the messenger, the protector-gone-rogue, or the societal influence? Perhaps all three?

- What goal will you conquer with your built-in Hack Codes of Visualization, Mental Rehearsal and the Reticular Activating System? I hope it's a juicy one that wakes you up with the Eye of the Tiger every morning!

- Which of the 10 people who MROYed (Maximize Return On You) inspired you to invest in your authenticity?

Now that you've exposed the enemy's playbook, it's time to fire the underperforming screenwriters and step up to direct your own masterpiece. You are rewiring your mind from pattern-driven behavior into The Director of Your Life. The contract is broken. It's time to sign your own movie deal.

The Universal Mandate: You Cannot Fail

Let me share the ultimate truth underpinning all achievement: winning is inevitable.

Success isn't about luck or random chance; it's governed by Universal Laws of Cause and Effect. If you input the correct steps, the Universe must return the desired output. This means achieving your goal, attaining your dream, is predictable and achievable if you apply these fundamental principles.

It boils down to a profound realization: **You Cannot Fail**. It's just a matter of time before you attain your desired outcome. So sit back and enjoy yourself.

My cousin Cynthi once gave me the clearest advice after I was denied a deeply desired position. She asked, "What would you do if you knew that you would get everything you wanted?" I immediately replied, "I'd chill out." "Exactly," she said. "You don't have to worry about how things look right now. The outcome is already guaranteed."

I offer you that same liberation. Don't worry if it doesn't look like you're going to run a sub 3:00 hour marathon. Don't worry if that cute girl or guy in the Marketing department hasn't asked you out yet. Trust that you have already put the essential elements into motion:

- You're doing the work.
- You're becoming a better, more elevated version of yourself every single day.

Guess what? With these elements in play, your victory is not a hope— it's a foregone conclusion. The Universe must follow your mandate and fulfill your desires.

Did We Tame the Dragon?

It all comes down to this: Why did you start? Why did you pick up this book and embark on this journey? It began with the simple, terrifying act of stepping into the spotlight—a single moment where you chose vulnerability over hiding.

I've been your guide to Outrun the Voice of Negativity, but the map I gave you was drawn from my own ultimate moment of terror.

Do you remember the story from the Preface? The exact instant this book was born? I had just finished recording a video, hitting 'publish' and exposing a vulnerable piece of myself to the world, when that monstrous voice—the one we've spent chapters dismantling—roared its ugly warning:

"Now you've done it. You've shown the world who you really are, and they're going to hate you."

That gut-punch of shame, that immediate regret, that desperate urge to delete the reels and retreat—that was the ultimate test of the Marathon Mindset. That was the choice between claiming my Ownership and retreating into the dark. I chose to blaze my frequency and live out loud, and that decision is the only reason this book is cradled in your hands right now. This is the moment where we prove that the dragon has been tamed, because the goal is to befriend your mind, not destroy it.

More than just the author guiding you from the sidelines, I have walked every kilometer of this mental race right alongside you. My commitment to the Marathon Mindset was immediately tested when a rapid succession of events forced these principles to move from abstract theory into necessary daily practice. This book stopped being a guide I was writing, and became the emergency toolkit I had to deploy daily. It forced me to not only practice every single principle I've preached but, in the process of surviving the turbulence, discover a few more necessary truths.

The Elevated Self: Beyond the Finish Line

It was this real-world crucible that made my communiques with some of the most legendary athletes in running even more impactful. Yes, I had the great fortune to interact with Billy Mills, Marshall Ulrich, Bart Yasso and John Kelly.

When we talk about John Kelly, we're talking about endurance royalty. The 41-year-old whose personal record requires a three-page scroll of logistics and suffering. He's not a self-promoter that gets the big media headlines, but to the hard-core endurance community, he is superhuman.

But here's the secret: Kelly's superpower isn't his lung capacity or his blistering pace; it's his holistic philosophy. The goal isn't just about winning a race, earning a new title, or finding the perfect relationship. It's about becoming a whole, elevated person—a more optimized version of yourself day by day. Kelly is constantly seeking a new summit, whether it's completing the Appalachian Trail with a personal best time or taking on the Tor des Géants in the Italian Alps. He perfectly embodies the philosophy of merging the three areas of life that matter most: Personal Mastery, Career Excellence, and Dedicated Relationships.

He's not just a hero on the trail; he's a hero in all three.

Now You Get to Be the Hero

The marathon is over, the blueprint for success is clear, and the lessons of the trail have been integrated into your new worldview. The legends showed us that the ultimate win is achieved not by surviving one event, but by integrating that same rigor into the fabric of your daily life. The goal is no longer to study the hero, but to become one. This is what I consider your Victory Lap, and it's time to claim it across your entire life.

The stakes for staying in the comfort zone of your old voice are high: you already know the sinking feeling of watching your life survive, rather than thrive. You know what it feels like to consume the garbage served up just to make you angry and divided. You've seen what failure looks and feels like.

The Call to Action is clear: Become the owner of the life you genuinely want to devour. The glorious movie you became the writer, director, and lead actor of is ready to unfold into an epic saga. You know the vision of success because you've met people who have escaped the voice, unplugged to restore, and become masters of their inner worlds.

You are now equipped with the fundamental rules of sovereignty. You know that you control your mind, and your mind is the most powerful tool you possess. You've retrained it to accept that you can create the reality you truly desire. The courage to split from the old tribe is the courage to stamp yourself into this new life. You know how to make friends with your mind, interrupt negativity, and make your inner world a safe place. You've learned that it takes a new, conscious program to train your mind into its rightful place: happiness.

Are you ready to embrace this new courage, break free from the spider-web of outworn patterns, and measure your success not just in steps, but in how completely you actualize your limitless potential?

The Finale

Alright, it's time. The finish line. The moment the physical agony melts away and all that's left is the intoxicating rush of accomplishment.

If you watch the Tour de France, you know that the final stage isn't a race; it's a coronation. After 21 brutal days, thousands of miles, and mountain climbs that defy gravity, the cyclists enter the ultimate victory lap through

Paris. The champion is already decided, their yellow jersey shining like a beacon, but this final ride—The Finale—is where they collect the emotional dividends on their impossible debt.

The energy is electric as they sweep onto the most famous boulevard in the world, the Champs-Élysées. Forget the pain, the crashes, and the sleepless nights; the mood shifts entirely from brutal competition to pure, collective triumph. The crowds are a deafening wall of sound. As they loop past the majestic Arc de Triomphe—a monument built to celebrate French military victories—the symbolism is perfect. They, too, have conquered.

The cyclists relax their shoulders for the first time in three weeks. They ride shoulder-to-shoulder, chatting, smiling, and sometimes even holding up glasses of champagne as they glide over the cobblestones. They have crossed their final finish line, not just against competitors, but against their own limits. This isn't about speed; it's about fully savoring the victory earned through grit, clarity, and quiet consistency. It is the moment they get to stop and feel how far they've come.

Your Victory Lap

The marathon is over, but the Marathon Mindset is not. It's not a program you finish; it is the supreme state you now occupy.

You are no longer reacting to the noise of the world, nor are you relying on luck or validation. You have claimed your role as Lead Actor, armed with the knowledge that your mind is your most powerful tool and your frequency is your most valuable asset.

This book was born from one critical moment of choice: to Blaze the signal of truth rather than shrink back into the comfort of fear. That same choice now sits before you every single morning. Your victory is assured because you are a 5 percenter—you dared to reject the ordinary, you mastered the science of your own happiness, and you accepted the universal mandate that you cannot fail.

So, step off the cobblestones of the Champs-Élysées. Let the roar of the crowd die down. The party is over, and the real life—your new life—is just beginning. Go forth and live with the profound, quiet confidence of someone who already knows they've won.

And finally, thank you for being brave with me.

Now go and enjoy your Victory Lap!

ACKNOWLEDGEMENTS

This book would not have been possible without the countless people who have made running a lifelong pursuit and generously shared their wisdom with me. Starting with my husband, Wayne Gibbons, whose insights, historical perspective, and deep-rooted experience—spanning five decades of running—brought invaluable depth to this work.

I am also deeply grateful to my editor Inessa Sage, who pulled a book out of me I never expected to write.

I'm a big fan of attribution, so I have included references, resources, and notes throughout this book plus fun notes about the people and ideas that shape the running world go round.

A big shout out to Dina Scacchetti and Tom Beatini, longtime runners and High Pointers who provided invaluable feedback on the OG chapter. Dina, thank you for the sports bra backstory. Tom, who generously shared his book collection, gave me a fashion show of his historic singlet collection, and shared the brilliant "nipple rot" phrase.

APPENDIX: RESOURCE AND REFERENCE GUIDE

I have curated the exercises, frameworks, and research from *Marathon Mindset: Outrun the Voice of Negativity* to help you bridge the gap between where you are and where you are destined to be.

Welcome to the community, Resilience Architect. Let's get to work. For a dynamic, regularly updated version of these tools, including exclusive video masterclasses, visit: RekhaGibbons.com/Resources

Gallery: The Digital Masterclass Series

Exclusive video interviews and deep dives into the athlete-executive mindset:

- *Mastering the Barkley Marathons*: An Interview with John Kelly on the mindset behind extreme endurance success. *Constrained Optimism*: A conversation on prioritizing family, high-stakes work, and elite performance.

- Marshall Ulrich: The Race isn't on the Pavement; It's between your Ears. Exclusive interview with Marshall Ulrich about how he developed his Marathon Mindset.

- Billy Mills. I had the great fortune to correspond with Mr. Mills, and his team. He graciously read the section featuring him and provided edits. Truly an honor to use Mr. Mills as a cultural legend that defeated the societal and personal demons that haunted him.

- *Old School Wisdom*: Bart Yasso on Lifetime Running Insights from the "Mayor of Running" with a focus on longevity and mental stamina.

- *The Plateau:* Insights from Amby Burfoot

References: OG History & Performance Research

Primary sources and deeper reading on the biological mechanisms of resilience:

- *Pedestrianism*: Davy Crockett's *Ultrarunning History* Podcast
- *When Shea Stadium Was More Than Baseball*
- *Sports Bra History: Jockstrap DNA*
- *The Winged Goddess Nike, Shoe Dog* by Phil Knight
- *Rule #5 – Velominati*, from *The Rules: The Way of the Cycling Disciple* — a compelling and often humorous perspective on discipline and mindset, even beyond cycling.
- *The Bannister Effect*: Shattering Impossible Limits

The Specialists in the Mindset Connection

- Anthony Astbury, founder of the Whole Man Academy
- Dr. Dennis Rebelo – *Story Like You Mean It*
- Arthur Lydiard, credited with coining the term "jogging"
- Norman Doidge – *The Brain That Changes Itself*
- Dr. David Hamilton, known for his work as a "Kindness Scientist"
- Brian Tracy, the Yoda of Responsibility
- Center for Humane Technology
- Dr. Anna Lembke – *Dopamine Nation*
- *Huberman Lab Podcast*—Dopamine and behavioral neuroscience
- Maria Zieja, ultrarunner and nature-based educator
- Chantal Zimmerman, founder of ANBE
- Lisa Davies–*Get the Edge UK*
- Kelly Howell, founder of Brainsync
- Dr. David Sinclair, researcher in longevity and aging science
- Paul Stamets, mycologist and advocate for medicinal mushrooms
- Vaz Sriharan, meditation programming and mental training

The Chemistry Behind Your Mindset Connection

Key concepts shaping the biological and behavioral foundations of mindset:

- Stress Response
- Negativity Default
- How Technology Has Wired Each Generation
- Doomscrolling
- Algorithm of Outrage
- Be an Owner, Not a Consumer
- Unplug to Restore
- Vagus Nerve
- Subconscious Reprogramming

MROY: Maximize Return on You

Case studies in investment, performance, and ROI

Profiles of individuals who exemplify high return on personal investment through discipline, resilience, and performance:

- MrBeast (James Stephen Donaldson)
- Kelly Lynn Adams
- Bart Yasso
- David Goggins
- Fred Schaeffer
- Chinazom Sunny Nwabueze
- Jasmin Paris
- John Kelly

The Resilience Architect's Toolkit

Practical tools, exercises, and frameworks designed to help you build and apply your Marathon Mindset:

- Superpower Finder
- Convergence Factor Equation
- Mindset Archetype Quiz
- Really Good Questions to Ask
- Architects of Anxiety: Inner Voice, Ego, and the Human Collective
- Runner's Brain vs. Doomscrolling
- Locus of Control Power Quiz
- 7 Ways to Be an Owner Checklist
- Altar of Overwhelm
- 4-Step Manifestation Plan
- The Monitor of Your Mind Remote Control
- TikTok Cat Filter: The Reticular Activating System
- Visualization: Immersive Forecasting
- The Vagus Waltz
- Framework for Your Future Self
- Lanternfly Stomp

www.ingramcontent.com/pod-product-compliance
Lightning Source LLC
Chambersburg PA
CBHW051516150726
47997CB00001B/275